THE POVERTY
OF PHILOSOPHY

THE POVERTY
OF PHILOSOPHY

KARL MARX

With an Introduction by

FREDERICK ENGELS

INTERNATIONAL PUBLISHERS
NEW YORK

PUBLISHER'S NOTE

This translation of Karl Marx's *The Poverty of Philosophy* has been made from the French edition of 1847. It takes into account the changes and corrections introduced by Marx into the copy presented to N. Utina in 1876, and also the corrections made by Frederick Engels for the second French edition and the German editions of 1885 and 1892.

All Rights Reserved, 1963
New edition, 1992

International Publishers, New York

Cover Illustration:
The Nike [Victory]
of Samothrace

Library of Congress Cataloging-in-Publication Data

Marx, Karl, 1818-1883.
    [Misère de la philosophie. English]
    The poverty of philosophy / Karl Marx ; with an introduction by
Frederick Engels. -- New ed.
        p.   cm.
    Translation of: Misère de la philosophie.
    Includes bibliographical references and index.
    ISBN 0-7178-0701-0 : $6.95
    1. Proudhon, P.-J. (Pierre-Joseph), 1809-1865. Systèmes des
contradictions économiques. 2. Marxian economics. I. Title.
HB163.P97M27913   1992
335.4'12--dc20   92-19799
                                                                       CIP

CONTENTS

PREFACE BY FREDERICK ENGELS

To the First German Edition

The present work was produced in the winter of 1846-47, at a time when Marx had cleared up for himself the basic features of his new historical and economic outlook. Proudhon's *Système des Contradictions économiques ou Philosophie de la Misère*, which had just appeared, gave him the opportunity to develop these basic features in opposing them to the views of a man who, from then on, was to occupy the chief place among living French Socialists. From the time when the two of them in Paris often spent whole nights in discussing economic questions, their paths had more and more diverged; Proudhon's book proved that there was already an unbridgeable gulf between them. To ignore it was at that time impossible, and so Marx by this answer of his put on record the irreparable rupture.

Marx's general opinion of Proudhon is to be found in the article,[1] given as appendix to this preface, which appeared in the Berlin *Sozialdemokrat*, Nos. 16, 17 and 18, in 1865. It was the only article that Marx wrote for that paper; Herr von Schweitzer's attempts, which soon afterwards became evident, to guide it along feudal and government lines compelled us to announce publicly the end of our collaboration after only a few weeks.

For Germany the present work has at this precise moment a significance which Marx himself never foresaw. How could he have known that, in trouncing Proudhon, he was hitting Rodbertus, the idol of the place hunters of today, whose very name was then unknown to him?

This is not the place to deal with the relation of Marx to Rodbertus; an opportunity for that is sure to occur to me very soon. Here it is sufficient to note that when Rodbertus accuses Marx of having "plundered" him and of having "freely used in his *Capital* without quoting him" his work *Zur Erkenntnis, etc.*, he permits himself a slander which is only explicable by the spleen of misunderstood genius and by his remarkable ignorance of things taking place outside Prussia, and especially of socialist

7

and economic literature. Neither these charges, nor the above-mentioned work of Rodbertus ever came to Marx's sight; all he knew of Rodbertus was the three *Soziale Briefe (Social Letters)* and even these certainly not before 1858 or 1859.

There is more basis for Rodbertus' assertion in these letters that he had already discovered "Proudhon's constituted value" *before* Proudhon; but here again it is true he erroneously flatters himself with being the *first* discoverer. In any case, he is for this reason covered by the criticism in the present work, and this compels me to deal briefly with his "fundamental" small work: *Zur Erkenntnis unsrer staatswirtschaftlichen Zustände (Contribution to the Knowledge of our National Economic Conditions)*, 1842, in so far as this brings forward anticipations of Proudhon as well as the communism of Weitling also (and again unconsciously) contained in it.

In so far as modern socialism, no matter of what tendency, starts out from bourgeois political economy, it almost exclusively links itself to the Ricardian theory of value. The two propositions which Ricardo proclaimed in 1817 right at the beginning of his *Principles,* 1) that the value of any commodity is purely and solely determined by the quantity of labour required for its production, and 2) that the product of the entire social labour is divided among the three classes: landowners (rent), capitalists (profit) and workers (wages), had ever since 1821 been utilized in England for socialist conclusions, and in part with such sharpness and decisiveness that this literature, which has now almost disappeared, and which to a large extent was first rediscovered by Marx, remained unsurpassed until the appearance of *Capital.* I will deal with this another time. If, therefore, in 1842, Rodbertus for his part drew socialist conclusions from the above propositions, that was certainly a very considerable step forward for a German at that time, but it was only for Germany that it could rank as a new discovery. That such an application of the Ricardian theory was far from new was proved by Marx against Proudhon who suffered from a similar conceit.

Anyone who is in any way familiar with the trend of political economy in England cannot fail to know that almost all the Socialists in this country have, at different periods, proposed the equalitarian application of the Ricardian theory. We could quote for M. Proudhon: Hodgskin, *Political Economy,* 1827; William Thompson, An *Inquiry into the Principles of the Distribution of Wealth Most Conducive to Human Happiness,* 1824; T. R. Edmonds, *Practical Moral and Political Economy,* 1828, etc., etc., and four pages more of *etc.* We shall content ourselves with listening to an English Communist, Mr. Bray ... in his remarkable work, *Labour's Wrongs and Labour's Remedy,* Leeds 1839.[2]

And the quotations given here from Bray alone put an end to a good part of the claim to priority made by Rodbertus.

At that time Marx had never yet been in the reading room of the British Museum. Besides the libraries of Paris and Brussels, besides my books and extracts seen during a six weeks' journey in England we made together in the summer of 1845, he had only examined such books as were obtainable in Manchester. The literature in question was, therefore, in the forties by no means so inaccessible as it may be now. If, all the same, it always remained unknown to Rodbertus, that is to be ascribed solely to his Prussian local narrowness. He is the real founder of specifically Prussian socialism and is now at last recognized as such.

However, even in his beloved Prussia, Rodbertus was not to remain undisturbed. In 1859, Marx's *Contribution to the Critique of Political Economy,* Part I, was published in Berlin. Therein, among the objections of the economists against Ricardo, was put forward as the second objection, p. 40:

> If the exchange value of a product is equal to the labour time which it contains, the exchange value of a labour day is equal to its product. Or the wage must be equal to the product of labour. But the contrary is the case:

On this there was the following note:

> This objection brought forward against Ricardo from the economic side was later taken up from the socialist side. The theoretical correctness of the formula being presupposed, practice was blamed for contradiction with theory and bourgeois society was invited to draw in practice the supposed conclusions from its theoretical principle. In this way at least, English Socialists turned the Ricardian formula of exchange value against political economy.

In the same note there was a reference to Marx's *Poverty of Philosophy,* which was then obtainable in all the bookshops.

Rodbertus, therefore, had sufficient opportunity of convincing himself whether his discoveries of 1842 were really new. Instead, he proclaims them again and again and regards them as so incomparable that it never comes into his head that Marx might have been able independently to draw his conclusions from Ricardo, just as well as Rodbertus himself. That was absolutely impossible! Marx had "plundered" him—him, whom the same Marx had offered every facility for convincing himself how long before both of them these conclusions, at least in the crude form which they still have in the case of Rodbertus, had been enunciated in England!

The simplest socialist application of the Ricardian theory is indeed that given above. It has led in many cases to insight into the origin and nature of surplus value which goes far beyond Ricardo, as in the case of Rodbertus among others. Apart from the fact that in this respect he nowhere presents anything which had not already been said before at least as well, his presentation suffers like those of his predecessors from the fact that he adopts, uncritically and without the least examination, the economic categories of labour, capital, value, etc., in the crude form, which clung to their external appearances, and in which they were handed down to him by the economists. He thereby not only cuts himself off from all further development—in contrast to Marx, who was the first to make something of these propositions so often repeated for the last sixty-four years—but, as will be shown, he opens for himself the road leading straight to utopia.

The above application of the Ricardian theory, that the entire social product belongs to the workers as *their* product, because they are the sole real producers, leads directly to communism. But, as Marx indicates too in the above-quoted passage, formally it is economically incorrect, for it is simply an application of morality to economics. According to the laws of bourgeois economics, the greatest part of the product does *not* belong to the workers who have produced it. If we now say: that is unjust, that ought not to be so, then that has nothing immediately to do with economics. We are merely saying that this economic fact is in contradiction to our sense of morality. Marx, therefore, never based his communist demands upon this, but upon the inevitable collapse of the capitalist mode of production which is daily taking place before our eyes to an ever greater degree; he says only that surplus value consists of unpaid labour, which is a simple fad. But what formally may be economically incorrect, may all the same be correct from the point of view of world history. If the moral consciousness of the mass declares an economic fact to be unjust, as it has done in the case of slavery or serf labour, that is a proof that the fact itself has been outlived, that other economic facts have made their appearance, owing to which the former has become unbearable and untenable. Therefore, a very true economic content may be concealed behind the formal economic incorrectness. This is not the place to deal more closely with the significance and history of the theory of surplus value.

At the same time other conclusions can be drawn, and have been drawn, from the Ricardian theory of value. The value of commodities is determined by the labour required for their production. It is found, however, that in this bad world commodities are sold sometimes above, sometimes below their value, and indeed not only as a result of variations in competition. The rate of profit has just as much the tendency to become equalized at the same level for all capitalists as the price of commodities has to become reduced to the labour value by the agency of supply and demand. But the rate of profit is calculated on the total capital invested in an industrial enterprise. Since now the annual product in two different branches of industry may incorporate equal quantities of labour, and, consequently, may represent equal values, and also wages may be equally high in both, while yet the capital invested in one branch may, and often is, twice or three times as great as in the other, consequently the Ricardian law of value, as Ricardo himself discovered, comes here into contradiction with the law of the equal rate of profit. If the products of both branches of industry are sold at their values, the rates of profit cannot be equal; if, however, the rates of profit are equal, then the products of both branches of industry certainly cannot always be sold at their values. Thus, we have here a contradiction, an antinomy of two economic laws, the practical solution of which takes place according to Ricardo (Chapter 1, Sections 4 and 5) as a rule in favour of the rate of profit at the cost of value.

But the Ricardian definition of value, in spite of its ominous characteristics, has a feature which makes it dear to the heart of the good bourgeois. It appeals with irresistible force to his sense of justice. Justice and equality of rights are the basic pillars on which the bourgeois of the eighteenth and nineteenth centuries would like to erect his social edifice over the ruins of feudal injustice, inequality and privilege. And the determination of the value of commodities by labour and the free exchange of the products of labour, taking place according to this measure of value between commodity owners with equal rights, these are, as Marx has already proved, the real bases on which the whole political, juridical and philosophical ideology of the modern bourgeoisie has been built. Once it is recognized that labour is the measure of value of a commodity, the better feelings of the good bourgeois cannot but be deeply wounded by the wickedness of a world which, while recognizing this basic law of justice in name, still in fact appears at every moment to set it aside without compunction. And the petty bourgeois especially, whose honest labour—even if it is only that of his workmen and apprentices—is daily more and more depreciated in value by the competition of large-scale production and machinery, this petty producer especially must long for a society in which the exchange of products according to their labour value is at last a complete and invariable truth. In other words, he is bound to long for a society in which a single law of commodity production prevails exclusively and in full, but where the conditions are abolished in which it can prevail at all, viz., the other laws of commodity production and, later, of capitalist production.

How deeply this utopia has struck roots in the mode of thought of the modern petty bourgeois—real or ideal—is proved by the fact that it was already systematically developed by John Gray in 1831, that it was tried in practice and theoretically widely preached in England in the thirties, that it was proclaimed as the latest truth by Rodbertus in Germany in 1842 and by Proudhon in France in 1846, that it was again proclaimed by Rodbertus even in 1871 as the solution of the social question and as, so to say, his social testament, and that in 1884 again it finds adherents among the horde of place hunters who in the name of Rodbertus set themselves to exploit Prussian state socialism.

The criticism of this utopia has been so exhaustively furnished by Marx both against Proudhon and against Gray (see the appendix to this work), that I can limit myself here to a few remarks on the form of proving and depicting it peculiar to Rodbertus.

As already said, Rodbertus adopts the traditional definitions of economic concepts entirely in the form in which they have come to him from the economists. He does not make the slightest attempt to investigate them. Value is for him "the valuation of one thing against others according to quantity, this valuation being conceived as measure." This, to put it mildly, extremely slovenly definition gives us at the best an idea of what value approximately looks like, but says absolutely nothing of what it is. Since this, however, is all that Rodbertus is able to tell us about value, it is comprehensible that he looks for a measure of value lying outside value. After thirty pages in which he mixes up use value and exchange value in higgledy-piggledy fashion with that power of abstract thought so infinitely admired by Herr Adolf Wagner, he arrives at the result that there is no real measure of value and that one has to make shift with a substitute measure. Labour can serve as such, but only if products of an equal quantity of labour are always exchanged against products of an equal quantity of labour; whether this "is already the case of itself, or whether measures are adopted" to ensure that it is. Consequently, value and labour remain without any sort of actual relation to each other, in spite of the fact that the whole first chapter is taken up to expound to us that commodities "cost labour" and nothing but labour, and why this is so.

Labour, again, is taken without examination in the form in which it occurs among the economists. And not even that. For,

although there is a reference in a couple of words to differences
in intensity of labour, labour is still put forward quite generally
as something which "costs," hence as something which measures
value, quite irrespective of whether it is expended under normal
average social conditions or not. Whether the producers use ten
days, or only one, for the preparation of products which could be
prepared in one day; whether they employ the best or the worst
tools; whether they expend their labour time in the production of
socially necessary articles and in the socially required quantity,
or whether they make quite undesired articles or desired articles
in quantities above or below the demand—about all this, there is
not a word: labour is labour, the product of equal labour must be
exchanged against the product of equal labour. Rodbertus, who is
otherwise always ready, whether rightly or not, to adopt the
national standpoint and to survey the relations of individual producers from the high watchtower of general social considerations,
carefully avoids doing so here. And this, indeed, solely because from
the very first line of his book he makes directly for the utopia of
labour money and because any investigation of labour in its property of producing value would be bound to put insuperable obstacles
in his way. His instinct was here considerably stronger than his
power of abstract thought, which, by the by, is revealed in Rodbertus by the most concrete absence of ideas.

The transition to utopia is now made in a hand's turn. The
"measures," which ensure exchange of commodities according to
labour value as the invariable rule, do not cause any difficulty.
The other utopians of this tendency, from Gray to Proudhon,
rack their brains to invent social institutions which would
achieve this aim. They attempt at least to solve the economic
question in an economic way through the action of the possessors
themselves who own the commodities to be exchanged. For Rodbertus it is much easier. As a good Prussian he appeals to the
state: a decree of the state power orders the reform.

In this way then, value is happily "constituted," but not by any
means the priority in this constitution which is claimed by Rodbertus. On the contrary, Gray as well as Bray—among many
others—before Rodbertus, often at length and to the point of
satiety, repeated this idea, viz., the pious desire for measures by
means of which products would always and under all circumstances be exchanged only at their labour value.

After the state has thus constituted value—at least for a part
of the products, for Rodbertus is also modest—it issues its labour
paper money, and gives advances therefrom to the industrial

capitalists, with which the latter pay the wages of the workers, whereupon the workers buy the products with the labour paper money they have received, and so cause the paper money to flow back to its starting point. How very beautifully this proceeds, one must hear from Rodbertus himself:

> In regard to the second condition, the necessary measure that the value certified in the note should be actually present in circulation is realized in that only the person who actually delivers a product receives a note, on which is accurately recorded the quantity of labour by which the product was produced. He who delivers a product of two days' labour receives a note marked "two days." By the strict observance of this rule in the issue of notes, the second condition too would necessarily be fulfilled. For as in accordance with our presuppositions the real value of the goods always coincides with the quantity of labour which their production has cost and this quantity of labour is measurable by the usual division of time, and therefore everyone who hands in a product on which two days' labour has been expended and receives a certificate for two days has received, certi- fied, or assigned to him, neither more nor less value than that which he has in fact supplied. Further, since *only* the person who has actually put a product into circulation receives such a certificate, it is equally certain that the value marked on the note. is available for the satisfaction of society. However extensive we imagine the circle of division of labour to be, if this rule is strictly followed *the sum total of available value must be exactly equal to the sum total of certified value.* Since, however, the total of certified value is exactly equal to the total of value assigned, the latter must *necessarily coincide with the available value, all claims will be satisfied and the liquidation correctly brought about.* (Pp. 166-67.)

If Rodbertus has hitherto always had the misfortune to arrive too late with his new discoveries, this time at least he has the merit of *one sort* of originality: none of his rivals has dared to express the stupidity of the labour money utopia in this child- ishly naive, transparent, I might say truly Pomeranian, form. Since for every paper certificate a corresponding object of value has been delivered, and no object of value is given out except against a corresponding paper certificate, the sum total of paper certificates must always be covered by the sum total of objects of value. The calculation works out without any remainder, it agrees down to a second of labour time, and no *Regierungs- Hauptkassen-Rentamtskalkulator*,[3] however grey in the service, could prove the slightest error in the reckoning. What more could one want?

In present-day capitalist society each industrial capitalist pro- duces on his own account what, how and as much as he likes. The social demand, however, remains an unknown magnitude to him, both in regard to quality, the kind of objects required, and in regard to quantity. That which today cannot be supplied quickly enough, may tomorrow be offered far in excess of the demand. Nevertheless, demand is finally satisfied in one way or another, well or badly, and, taken as a whole, production is finally directed towards the objects required. How is this reconciliation of the contradiction effected? By competition. And how does competition bring about this solution? Simply by depreciating below their labour value those commodities which in kind or amount are useless for immediate social requirements, and by making the producers feel, through this roundabout means, that they have produced either absolutely useless articles or useful articles in unusable, superfluous quantity. From this, two things follow.

First, the continual deviation of the prices of commodities from their values is the necessary condition in and through which alone the value of the commodities can come into existence. Only through the fluctuations of competition, and consequently of commodity prices, does the law of value of commodity production assert itself and the determination of the value of the commodity by the socially necessary labour time become a reality. That thereby the form of manifestation of value, the price, as a rule has a different aspect from the value which it manifests, is a fate which value shares with most social relations. The king usually looks quite different from the monarchy that he represents. To desire, in a society of producers who exchange their commodities, to establish the determination of value by labour time, by forbidding competition to establish this determination of value through pressure on prices in the only way in which it can be established, is therefore merely to prove that, at least in this sphere, one has adopted the usual utopian disdain of economic laws.

Secondly, competition, by bringing into operation the law of value of commodity production in a society of producers who exchange their commodities, precisely thereby brings about the only organization and arrangement of social production which is possible in the circumstances. Only through the undervaluation or overvaluation of products is it forcibly brought home to the individual commodity producers what things and what quantity of them society requires or does not require. But it is just this sole regulator that the utopia in which Rodbertus also shares would abolish. And if we then ask what guarantee we have that necessary quantity and not more of each product will be produced, that we shall not go hungry in regard to corn and meat while we are choked in beet sugar and drowned in potato spirit, that we shall not lack trousers to cover our nakedness while trouser buttons flood us in millions—Rodbertus triumphantly shows us his famous calculation, according to which the correct certificate has been handed out for every superfluous pound of sugar, for every unsold barrel of spirit, for every unusable trouser button, a calculation which "works out" exactly, and according to which "all claims will be satisfied and the liquidation correctly brought about." And any-one who does not believe this can apply to the governmental chief revenue office accountant, X, in Pomerania, who has supervised the calculation and found it correct and who, as one who has never yet been found guilty of a mistake in his cash account, is thoroughly trustworthy.

And now consider the naiveté with which Rodbertus would abolish industrial and trade crises by means of his utopia. As soon as the production of commodities has assumed world market dimensions, the equalization between the individual producers who produce for private account and the market for which they produce, which in respect of quantity and quality of demand is more or less unknown to them, is established by means of a storm in the world market, by a trade crisis.* If now competition is to be forbidden to make the individual producers aware, by the rise or fall of prices, how the world market stands, then their eyes are completely blinded. To institute the production of commodities in such a fashion that the producers cannot any more learn anything about the state of the market for which they are producing—that indeed is a cure for the disease of crisis which could make Dr. Eisenbart envious of Rodbertus.

(One now comprehends why Rodbertus determines the value of commodities simply by "labour" and at most admits of different degrees of intensity of labour. If he had investigated by what means and how labour creates value and therefore also determines and measures it, he would have arrived at socially necessary labour, necessary for the single product, both in relation to other products of the same kind and also in relation to society's total demand. He would thereby be confronted with the question how the adjustment of the production of separate commodity producers to the total social demand takes place, and his whole utopia would thereby have been made impossible. This time he

---

* At least, this was the case until recently. Since England's monopoly of the world market is being more and more shattered by the participation of France, Germany and, above all, of America in world trade, a new form of equalization appears to be operating. The period of general prosperity preceding the crisis still fails to appear. If it should fail altogether, then chronic stagnation would necessarily become the normal condition of modern industry, with only insignificant fluctuations. [Note by F. Engels.]

preferred in fact to "make an abstraction," namely of precisely that which mattered.

Now at last we come to the point where Rodbertus really offers us something new; something which distinguishes him from all his numerous fellow supporters of labour money exchange economy. They all demand this exchange organization with the aim of abolishing the exploitation of wage labour by capital. Every producer is to receive the full labour value of his product. In this they all agree, from Gray to Proudhon. Not at all, says Rodbertus. Wage labour and its exploitation remains.

In the first place, in no conceivable state of society can the worker receive for consumption the entire value of his product. A series of economically unproductive but necessary functions have to be met from the fund produced, and consequently also the persons connected with them maintained. This is only correct so long as the present-day division of labour holds. In a society in which general productive labour is obligatory, which is, however, also "conceivable," this falls to the ground. But the necessity for a fund for social reserve and accumulation would remain and consequently even in that case, while the workers as a whole, i.e., all, would remain in possession and enjoyment of their total product, each separate worker would not enjoy the "full product of his labour." Nor has the maintenance of economically unproductive functions at the expense of the labour product been overlooked by the other labour money utopians. But they leave the workers to tax themselves for this purpose in the usual democratic way, while Rodbertus, whose whole social reform of 1842 is adapted to the Prussian state of that time, refers the whole matter to the decision of the bureaucracy, which determines from above the share of the worker in his own product and graciously permits him to have it.

In the second place, ground rent and profit are also to continue undiminished. For the landowners and industrial capitalists also exercise certain socially useful or even necessary functions, even if economically unproductive ones, and they receive in the shape of ground rent and profit a sort of pay on that account—a conception which was admittedly not new even in 1842. Actually they get at present far too much for the little that they do, and do badly enough, but Rodbertus has need, at least for the next five hundred years, of a privileged class, and so the present rate of surplus value, to express myself correctly is to remain in existence but is not to be allowed to be increased. This present rate of surplus value Rodbertus takes to be two hundred per cent, that is to say, for twelve hours of labour daily the worker is to receive a certificate not for twelve hours but for only four, and the value produced in the remaining eight hours is to be divided between landowner and capitalist. The labour certificates of Rodbertus, therefore, directly lie. Again, one must be a Pomeranian Junker in order to imagine that a working class would put up with working twelve hours in order to receive a certificate of four hours of labour. If the hocus-pocus of capitalist production is translated into this naive language, in which it appears as naked robbery, it is made impossible. Every certificate given to a worker would be a direct instigation to rebellion and would come under § 110 of the German Imperial Penal Code. One must never have seen any other proletariat than the day-labourer proletariat, still actually in semi-serfdom, of a Pomeranian Junker's estate, where the rod and the whip reign supreme, and where all the good-looking women of the village belong to his lordship's harem, in order to imagine one can offer such an insult to the workers. But our conservatives are just our greatest revolutionaries.

If, however, our workers are sufficiently docile to suffer the imposition that they have in reality only worked four hours after twelve whole hours of hard labour, they are, as a reward, to be guaranteed that for all eternity their share in their own product will never fall below a third. That is indeed music of the future played on a child's trumpet and not worth wasting a word over. Therefore, insofar as there is anything novel in the labour money exchange utopia of Rodbertus, this novelty is simply childish and far below the achievements of his numerous comrades both before and after him.

For the time when Rodbertus' *Zur Erkenntnis, etc.,* appeared, it was certainly an important book. His development of Ricardo's theory of value in one direction was a very promising beginning. Even if it was only for him and for Germany that it was new, still as a whole, it stands on an equal level with the achievements of the better of his English predecessors. But it was only a beginning, from which a real gain for theory could be achieved only by further thorough and critical work. But he cut himself off from further development in this direction by also developing Ricardo's theory from the very beginning in the second direction, in the direction of utopia. Thereby he lost the first condition of all criticism—freedom from bias. He worked on towards a goal fixed in advance, he became a *Tendenzökonom.*[4]

Once caught in the toils of his utopia, he cut himself off from all possibility of scientific advance. From 1842 up to his death, he went round in a circle, always repeating the same ideas which he had already expressed or indicated in his first work, feeling himself unappreciated, finding himself plundered, where there was nothing to plunder, and at last refusing, not without deliberate intention, to recognize that at bottom he had only rediscovered what had already been discovered long before.

*   *   *

In a few places the translation departs from the printed French original. This is based on alterations in Marx's own handwriting, which will also be inserted in the new French edition now being prepared.

It is hardly necessary to point out that the terminology used in this work does not quite coincide with that in *Capital*. Thus this work still speaks of *labour* as a commodity, of the purchase and sale of labour, instead of *labour power*.

In this edition there is also added as a supplement: 1) a passage from Marx's work *Zur Kritik der politischen Ökonomie [A Contribution to the Critique of Political Economy]*, Berlin 1859, dealing with the first labour money exchange utopia of John Gray, and 2) a translation of Marx's speech on free trade in Brussels (1848), which belongs to the same period of development of the author as the *Poverty*.

Frederick Engels

London, October 23, 1884

PREFACE TO THE SECOND GERMAN EDITION

For the second edition I have only to remark that the name wrongly written Hopkins in the French text (on page 45[5]) has been replaced by the correct name Hodgskin and that in the same place the date of the work of William Thompson has been corrected to 1824. It is to be hoped that this will appease the bibliographical conscience of Professor Anton Menger.

Frederick Engels

London, March 29, 1892

KARL MARX

THE POVERTY OF PHILOSOPHY
Answer to the Philosophy of Poverty
by M. Proudhon[6]

FOREWORD

M. Proudhon has the misfortune of being peculiarly misunderstood in Europe. In France, he has the right to be a bad economist, because he is reputed to be a good German philosopher. In Germany, he has the right to be a bad philosopher, because he is reputed to be one of the ablest of French economists. Being both German and economist at the same time, we desire to protest against this double error.

The reader will understand that in this thankless task we have often had to abandon our criticism of M. Proudhon in order to criticize German philosophy, and at the same time to give some observations on political economy.

Karl Marx

Brussels, June 15, 1847

M. Proudhon's work is not just a treatise on political economy, an ordinary book; it is a bible. "Mysteries," "Secrets Wrested from the Bosom of God," "Revelations"—it lacks nothing. But as prophets are discussed nowadays more conscientiously than profane writers, the reader must resign himself to going with us through the arid and gloomy erudition of "Genesis," in order to ascend later, with M. Proudhon, into the ethereal and fertile realm of *super-socialism*. (See Proudhon, *Philosophy of Poverty*, Prologue, p. III, line 20.)

CHAPTER I

A SCIENTIFIC DISCOVERY

§1. THE ANTITHESIS OF USE VALUE AND EXCHANGE VALUE

> The capacity of all products, whether natural or industrial, to contribute to man's subsistence is specifically termed *use value;* their capacity to be given in exchange for one another, *exchange value....* How does use value become exchange value? ... The genesis of the idea of (exchange) value has not been noted by -economists with sufficient care. It is necessary, therefore, for us to dwell upon it. Since a very large number of the things I need occur in nature only in moderate quantities, or even not at all, I am forced to assist in the production of what I lack. And as I cannot set my hand to so many things, I shall *propose* to other men, my collaborators in various functions, to cede to me a part of their products in *exchange* for mine. (Proudhon, Vol. 1, Chap. II.)

M. Proudhon undertakes to explain to us first of all the double nature of value, the *"distinction in value,"* the process by which use value is transformed into exchange value. It is necessary for us to dwell with M. Proudhon upon this act of transubstantiation. The following is how this act is accomplished, according to our author.

A very large number of products are not to be found in nature, they are products of industry. If man's needs go beyond nature's spontaneous production, he is forced to have recourse to industrial production. What is this industry in M. Proudhon's view? What is its origin? A single individual, feeling the need for a very great number of things, "cannot set his hand to so many things." So many needs to satisfy presuppose so many things to produce—there are no products without production. So many things to produce presuppose at once more than one man's hand helping to produce them. Now, the moment you postulate more than one hand helping in production, you at once presuppose a whole production based on the division of labour. Thus need, as M. Proudhon presupposes it, itself presupposes the whole division of labour. In presupposing the division of labour, you get exchange, and, consequently, exchange value. One might as well have presupposed exchange value from the very beginning.

But M. Proudhon prefers to go the roundabout way. Let us follow him in all his detours, which always bring him back to his starting point.

In order to emerge from the condition in which everyone produces in isolation and to arrive at exchange, "I turn to my collaborators in various functions," says M. Proudhon. I myself, then, have collaborators, all with different functions. And yet, for all that, I and all the others, always according to M. Proudhon's supposition, have got no farther than the solitary and hardly social position of the Robinsons. The collaborators and the various functions, the division of labour and the exchange it implies, are already to hand.

To sum up: I have certain needs which are founded on the division of labour and on exchange. In presupposing these needs, M. Proudhon has thus presupposed exchange, exchange value, the very thing of which he purposes to "note the genesis with more care than other economists."

M. Proudhon might just as well have inverted the order of things, without in any way affecting the accuracy of his conclusions. To explain exchange value, we must have exchange. To explain exchange, we must have the division of labour. To explain the division of labour, we must have needs which render necessary the division of labour. To explain these needs, we must *"Presuppose"* them, which is not to deny them—contrary to the first axiom in M. Proudhon's prologue: "To presuppose God is to deny Him" (Prologue, p. 1).

How does M. Proudhon, who assumes the division of labour as the known, manage to explain exchange value, which for him is always the unknown?

"A man" sets out to *"propose* to other men, his collaborators in various functions," that they establish exchange, and make a distinction between ordinary value and exchange value. In accepting this proposed distinction, the collaborators have left M. Proudhon no other "care" than that of recording the fact, of marking, of "noting" in his treatise on political economy "the genesis of the idea of value." But he has still to explain to us the "genesis" of this proposal, to tell us finally how this single individual, this Robinson, suddenly had the idea of making "to his collaborators" a proposal of the type *known* and how these collaborators accepted it without the slightest protest.

M. Proudhon does not enter into these genealogical details. He merely places a sort of historical stamp upon the fact of exchange, by presenting it in the form of a motion, made by a third party, that exchange be established.

That is a sample of the *"historical and descriptive method"* of M. Proudhon, who professes a superb disdain for the "historical and descriptive methods" of the Adam Smiths and Ricardos.

Exchange has a history of its own. It has passed through different phases.

There was a time, as in the Middle Ages, when only the superfluous, the excess of production over consumption, was exchanged.

There was again a time, when not only the superfluous, but all products, all industrial existence, had passed into commerce, when the whole of production depended on exchange. How are we to explain this second phase of exchange-marketable value at its second power?

M. Proudhon would have a reply ready-made: Assume that a man has *"proposed* to other men, his collaborators in various functions," to raise marketable value to its second power.

Finally, there came a time when everything that men had considered as inalienable became an object of exchange, of traffic and could be alienated. This is the time when the very things which till then had been communicated, but never exchanged; given, but never sold; acquired, but never bought—virtue, love, conviction, knowledge, conscience, etc.—when everything, in short, passed into commerce. It is the time of general corruption, of universal venality, or, to speak in terms of political economy, the time when everything, moral or physical, having become a marketable value, is brought to the market to be assessed at its truest value.

How, again, can we explain this new and last phase of exchange—marketable value at its third power?

M. Proudhon would have a reply ready-made: Assume that a person has *"proposed* to other persons, his collaborators in various functions," to make a marketable value out of virtue, love, etc., to raise exchange value to its third and last power.

We see that M. Proudhon's "historical and descriptive method" is applicable to everything, it answers everything, explains everything. If it is a question above all of explaining historically "the genesis of an economic idea," it postulates a man who proposes to other men, "his collaborators in various functions," that they perform this act of genesis and that is the end of it.

We shall hereafter accept the "genesis" of exchange value as an accomplished act; it now remains only to expound the relation between exchange value and use value. Let us hear what M. Proudhon has to say:

Economists have very well brought out the double character of value, but what they have not pointed out with the same precision is its *contradictory nature;* this is where our criticism begins.... It is a small thing to have drawn attention to this surprising contrast between use value and exchange value, in which economists have been wont to see only something very simple: we must show that this alleged simplicity conceals a profound mystery into which it is our duty to penetrate.... In technical terms, use value and exchange value stand in inverse ratio to each other.

If we have thoroughly grasped M. Proudhon's thought the following are the four points which he sets out to establish:

1. Use value and exchange value form a "surprising contrast," they are in opposition to each other.

2. Use value and exchange value are in inverse ratio, in contradiction, to each other.

3. Economists have neither observed nor recognized either the opposition or the contradiction.

4. M. Proudhon's criticism begins at the end.

We, too, shall begin at the end, and, in order to clear the economists from M. Proudhon's accusations, we shall let two sufficiently well-known economists speak for themselves.

Sismondi: "It is the opposition between use value and exchange value to which commerce has reduced everything, etc. *(Etudes,* Volume II, p. 162, Brussels edition.)

Lauderdale: "In proportion as the riches of individuals are increased by an augmentation of the value of any commodity, the wealth of the society is generally diminished; and in proportion as the mass of individual riches is diminished, by the diminution of the value of any commodity, its opulence is generally increased." *(Recherches sur la nature et l'origine de la richesse publique;* translated by Langentie de Lavaïsse. Paris 1808 [p. 33].)

Sismondi founded on the *opposition* between use value and exchange value his principal doctrine, according to which diminution in revenue is proportional the increase in production.

Lauderdale founded his system on the inverse ratio of the two kinds of value, and his doctrine was indeed so popular in Ricardo's time that the latter could speak of it as of something generally known. "It is through confounding the ideas of value and wealth, or riches that it has been asserted, that by diminishing the quantity of commodities, that is to say, of the necessaries conveniences, and enjoyments of human life, riches may be increased." (Ricardo, *Principes de l'économie politique,* translated by Constancio, annotations by J. B. Say. Paris 1835; Volume II, chapter *Sur la valeur et les richesses.*)

We have just seen that the economists before M. Proudhon had "drawn attention" to the profound mystery of opposition and contradiction. Let us now see how M. Proudhon in his turn explains this mystery after the economists.

The exchange value of a product falls as the supply increases, the demand remaining the same; in other words, the more abundant a product is *relatively to the demand*, the lower is its exchange value, or price. *Vice versa:* The weaker the supply relatively to the demand, the higher rises the exchange value of the price of the product supplied: in other words, the greater the scarcity in the products supplied, relatively to the demand, the higher the prices. The exchange value of a product depends upon its abundance or its scarcity, but always in relation to the demand. Take a product that is more than scarce, unique of its kind if you will: this unique product will be more than abundant, it will be superfluous, if there is no demand for it. On the other hand, take a product multiplied into millions, it will always be scarce if it does not satisfy the demand, that is, if there is too great a demand for it.

These are what we should almost call truisms, yet we have had to repeat them here in order to render M. Proudhon's mysteries comprehensible.

> So that, following up the principle to its ultimate consequences, one would come to the conclusion, the most logical in the world, that the things whose use is indispensable and whose quantity is unlimited should be had for nothing, and those whose utility is nil and whose scarcity is extreme should be of incalculable worth. To cap the difficulty, these extremes are impossible in practice: on the one hand, no human product could ever be unlimited in magnitude; on the other, even the scarcest things must perforce be useful to a certain degree, otherwise they would be quite valueless. Use value and exchange value are thus inexorably bound up with each other, although by their nature they continually tend to be mutually exclusive. (Volume I, p. 39.)

What caps M. Proudhon's difficulty? That he has simply forgotten about *demand*, and that a thing can be scarce or abundant only in so far as it is in demand. The moment he leaves out demand, he identifies exchange value with *scarcity* and use value with *abundance*. In reality, in saying that things "whose *utility is nil and scarcity extreme* are of *incalculable worth*," *he* is simply declaring that exchange value is merely scarcity. "Scarcity extreme and utility nil" means pure scarcity. "Incalculable worth" is the maximum of exchange value, it is pure exchange value. He equates these two terms. Therefore exchange value and scarcity are equivalent terms. In arriving at these alleged "extreme consequences," M. Proudhon has in fact carried to the extreme, not the things, but the terms which express them, and, in so doing, he shows proficiency in rhetoric rather than in logic. He merely rediscovers his first hypotheses in all their nakedness, when he thinks he has discovered new consequences. Thanks to the same procedure he succeeds in identifying use value with pure abundance.

After having equated exchange value and scarcity, use value and abundance, M. Proudhon is quite astonished not to find use value in scarcity and exchange value, nor exchange value in abundance and use value; and seeing that these extremes are impossible in practice, he can do nothing but believe in mystery. Incalculable worth exists for him, because buyers do not exist, and he will never find any buyers, so long as he leaves out demand.

On the other hand, M. Proudhon's abundance seems to be something spontaneous. He completely forgets that there are people who produce it, and that it is to their interest never to lose sight of demand. Otherwise, how could M. Proudhon have said that things which are very useful must have a very low price, or even cost nothing? On the contrary, he should have concluded that abundance, the production of very useful things, should be restricted if their price, their exchange value, is to be raised. The old vine-growers of France in petitioning for a law to forbid the planting of new vines; the Dutch in burning Asiatic spices, in uprooting clove trees in the Moluccas, were simply trying to reduce abundance in order to raise exchange value. During the whole of the Middle Ages this same principle was acted upon, in limiting by laws the number of journeymen a single master could employ and the number of implements he could use. (See Anderson, *History of Commerce.**)

After having represented abundance as use value and scarcity as exchange value—nothing indeed is easier than to prove that abundance and scarcity are in inverse ratio—M. Proudhon identifies use value with *supply* and exchange value with *demand.* To make the antithesis even more clear-cut, he substitutes a new term, putting *"estimation value"* instead of *exchange value.* The battle has now shifted its ground, and we have on one side *utility* (use value, supply), on the other, *estimation* (exchange value, demand).

* A. Anderson, *An Historical and Chronological Deduction of the Origin of Commerce from the Earliest Accounts to the Present Time.* First edition appeared in London in 1764.

Who is to reconcile these two contradictory forces? What is to be done to bring them into harmony with each other? Is it possible to find in them even a single point of comparison?

Certainly, cries M. Proudhon, there is one—*free will*. The price resulting from this battle between supply and demand, between utility and estimation will not be the expression of eternal justice.

M. Proudhon goes on to develop this antithesis.

> In my capacity as a *free buyer*, I am judge of my needs, judge of the desirability of an object, judge of the price *I am willing* to pay for it. On the other hand, in your capacity as a *free producer*, you are master of the *means of execution*, and in consequence, you have the power to reduce your expenses. (Volume I, p. 41.)

And as demand, or exchange value, is identical with estimation, M. Proudhon is led to say:

> It is proved that it is man's *free will* that gives rise to the opposition between use value and exchange value. How can this opposition be removed, so long as free will exists? And how can the latter be sacrificed without sacrificing mankind? (Volume I, p. 41.)

Thus there is no possible way out. There is a struggle between two as it were incommensurable powers, between utility and estimation, between the free buyer and the free producer.

Let us look at things a little more closely.

Supply does not represent exclusively utility, demand does not represent exclusively estimation. Does not the demander also supply a certain product or the token representing all products, viz., money; and as supplier, does he not represent, according to M. Proudhon, utility or use value?

Again, does not the supplier also demand a certain product or the token representing all products, viz., money? And does he not thus become the representative of estimation, of estimation value or of exchange value?

Demand is at the same time a supply, supply is at the same time a demand. Thus M. Proudhon's antithesis, in simply identifying supply and demand, the one with utility, the other with estimation, is based only on a futile abstraction.

What M. Proudhon calls use value is called estimation value by other economists, and with just as much right. We shall quote only Storch (*Cours d'économie politique*, Paris 1823, pp. 48 and 49).

According to him, *needs* are the things for which we feel the need; *values* are things to which we attribute value. Most things have value only because they satisfy needs engendered by esti-

mation. The estimation of our needs may change; therefore the
utility of things, which expresses only the relation of these things
to our needs, may also change. Natural needs themselves are
continually changing. Indeed, what could be more varied than
the objects which form the staple food of different peoples!

The conflict does not take place between utility and estimation; it takes place between the marketable value demanded by
the supplier and the marketable value supplied by the demander. The exchange value of the product is each time the resultant
of these contradictory appreciations.

In final analysis, supply and demand bring together production and consumption, but production and consumption based on
individual exchanges.

The product supplied is not useful in itself. It is the consumer
who determines its utility. And even when its quality of being
useful is admitted, it does not exclusively represent utility. In
the course of production, it has been exchanged for all the costs
of production, such as raw materials, wages of workers, etc., all
of which are marketable values. The product, therefore, represents, in the eyes of the producer, a sum total of marketable
values. What he supplies is not only a useful object, but also and
above all a marketable value.

As to demand, it will only be effective on condition that it has
means of exchange at its disposal. These means are themselves
products, marketable value.

In supply and demand, then, we find, on the one hand, a
product which has cost marketable values, and the need to sell;
on the other, means which have cost marketable values, and the
desire to buy.

M. Proudhon opposes the *free buyer* to the *free producer*. To
the one and to the other he attributes purely metaphysical qualities. It is this that makes him say: "It is proved that it is man's
free will that gives rise to the opposition between use value and
exchange value." [I: 41] The producer, the moment he produces
in a society founded on the division of labour and on exchange
(and that is M. Proudhon's hypothesis), is forced to sell. M.
Proudhon makes the producer master of the means of production; but he will agree with us that his means of production do
not depend on *free will*. Moreover, many of these means of production are products which he gets from the outside, and in
modern production he is not even free to produce the amount he
wants. The actual degree of development of the productive forces
compels him to produce on such or such a scale.

The consumer is no freer than the producer. His judgment depends on his means and his needs. Both of these are determined by his social position, which itself depends on the whole social organization. True, the worker who buys potatoes and the kept woman who buys lace both follow their respective judgments. But the difference in their judgments is explained by the difference in the positions they occupy in the world, and which themselves are the product of social organization.

Is the entire system of needs founded on estimation or on the whole organization of production? Most often, needs arise directly from production or from a state of affairs based on production. World trade turns almost entirely round the needs, not of individual consumption, but of production. Thus, to choose another example, does not the need for lawyers suppose a given civil law which is but the expression of a certain development of property, that is to say, of production?

It is not enough for M. Proudhon to have eliminated the elements just mentioned from the relation of supply and demand. He carries abstraction to the furthest limits when he fuses all producers into *one single* producer, all consumers into *one single* consumer, and sets up a struggle between these two chimerical personages. But in the real world, things happen otherwise. The competition among the suppliers and the competition among the demanders form a necessary part of the struggle between buyers and sellers, of which marketable value is the result.

After having eliminated competition and the cost of production, M. Proudhon can at his ease reduce the formula of supply and demand to an absurdity.

"Supply and demand," he says, "are merely two *ceremonial forms* that serve to bring use value and exchange value face to face, and to lead to their reconciliation. They are the two electric poles which, when connected, must produce the phenomenon of affinity called ex*change*." (I: 49, 50.)

One might as well say that exchange is merely a "ceremonial form" for introducing the consumer to the object of consumption. One might as well say that all economic relations are "ceremonial forms" serving immediate consumption as go-betweens. Supply and demand are neither more nor less relations of a given production than are individual exchanges.

What, then, does all M. Proudhon's dialectic consist in? In the substitution for use value and exchange value, for supply and demand, of abstract and contradictory notions like scarcity and abundance, utility and estimation, *one* producer and *one* consumer, both of them *knights of free will.*

And what was he aiming at?

At arranging for himself a means of introducing later on one of the elements he had set aside, the *cost of production,* as the *synthesis* of use value and exchange value. And it is thus that in his eyes the cost of production constitutes *synthetic value or constituted value.*

§2. CONSTITUTED VALUE OR SYNTHETIC VALUE

"Value (marketable value) is the cornerstone of the economic structure." *"Constituted"* value is the cornerstone of the system of economic contradictions.

M. What then is this *"constituted value"* which is all Proudhon has discovered in political economy?

Once utility is admitted, labour is the source of value. The measure of labour is time. The relative value of products is determined by the labour time required for their production. Price is the monetary expression of the relative value of a product. Finally, the *constituted value* of a product is purely and simply the value which is constituted by the labour time incorporated in it.

Just as Adam Smith discovered the *division of labour,* so he, M. Proudhon, claims to have discovered *"constituted value."* This is not exactly "something unheard of," but then it must be admitted that there is nothing unheard of in any discovery of economic science. M. Proudhon, who appreciates to the full the importance of his own invention, seeks nevertheless to tone down the merit thereof "in order to reassure the reader as to his claims to originality, and to win over minds whose timidity renders them little favourable to new ideas." But in apportioning the contribution made by each of his predecessors to the understanding of value, he is forced to confess openly that the largest portion, the lion's share, of the merit falls to himself.

> The synthetic idea of value had been vaguely perceived by Adam Smith....
> But with Adam Smith this idea of value was entirely intuitive. Now,
> society does not change its habits merely on the strength of intuitions: its
> decisions are made only on the authority of facts. The antinomy had to be
> stated more palpably and more clearly: J. B. Say was its chief interpreter.
> [I: 66]

Here, in a nutshell, is the history of the discovery of synthetic value: Adam Smith—vague intuition; J. B. Say—antinomy; M. Proudhon—constituting and "constituted" truth. And let there be no mistake about it: all the other economists, from Say to Proudhon, have merely been trudging along in the rut of antinomy.

> It is incredible that for the last forty years so many men of sense should
> have fumed and fretted at such a simple idea. But no, *values are compared*

without there being any point of comparison between them and with no unit of measurements; this, rather than embrace the revolutionary theory of equality, is what *the economists of the nineteenth century* are resolved to uphold against all comers. *What will posterity say about it?* (I: 68).

Posterity, so abruptly invoked, will begin by getting muddled over the chronology. It is bound to ask itself: are not Ricardo and his school economists of the nineteenth century? Ricardo's system, putting as a principle that "the relative value of commodities corresponds exclusively to the amount of labour required for their production," dates from 1817.[7] Ricardo is the head of a whole school dominant in England since the Restoration.[8] The Ricardian doctrine summarizes severely, remorselessly, the whole of the English bourgeoisie, which is itself the type of the modern bourgeoisie. "What will posterity say about it?" It will not say that M. Proudhon did not know Ricardo, for he talks about him, he talks at length about him, he keeps coming back to him, and concludes by calling his system "trash." If ever posterity does interfere, it will say perhaps that M. Proudhon, afraid of offending his readers' Anglophobia, preferred to make himself the responsible editor of Ricardo's ideas. In any case, it will think it very naive that M. Proudhon should give as a "revolutionary theory of the future" what Ricardo expounded scientifically as the theory of present-day society, of bourgeois society, and that he should thus take for the solution of the antinomy between utility and exchange value what Ricardo and his school presented long before him as the scientific formula of one single side of this antinomy, that of *exchange value.* But let us leave posterity alone once and for all, and confront M. Proudhon with his predecessor Ricardo. Here are some extracts from this author which summarize his doctrine on value:

Utility then is not the measure of *exchangeable* value, although it is absolutely essential to it. (Vol. I, p. 3, *Principes de l'économie politique,* etc., translated from the English by F. S. Constancio, Paris 1835.)

Possessing utility, commodities derive their exchangeable value from two sources: from their scarcity, and from the quantity of labour required to obtain them. There are some commodities, the value of which is determined by their scarcity alone. No labour can increase the quantity of such goods, and therefore their value cannot be lowered by an increased supply. Some rare statues and pictures, scarce books ... are all of this description. Their value ... varies with the varying wealth and inclinations of those who are desirous to possess them. (Vol. I, pp. 4 and 5, *l. c.*) These commodities, however, form a very small part of the mass of commodities daily exchanged in the market. By far the greatest part of those goods which are the objects of desire, are procured by labour; and they may be multiplied, not in one country alone, but in many, almost without any assignable limit, if we are disposed to bestow the labour necessary to obtain them. (Vol. I, p.

5, *l. c.*) In speaking then of commodities, of their exchangeable value, and of the laws which regulate their relative prices, we mean always such commodities only as can be increased in quantity by the exertion of human industry, and on the production of which competition operates without restraint. (Vol. I, p. 5.)

Ricardo quotes Adam Smith, who, according to him, *so accurately* defined the original source of exchangeable value" (Adam Smith, *Wealth of Nations,* Book I, Chap. 5[9]) , and he adds:

That this (i.e., labour time) is really the foundation of the exchangeable value of all things, excepting those which cannot be increased by human industry, is a doctrine of the utmost importance in political economy; for from no source do so many errors, and so much difference of opinion in that science proceed, as from the vague ideas which are attached to the word *value."* (Vol. I, p. 8.) "If the quantity of labour realized in commodities regulate their exchangeable value, every increase of the quantity of labour must augment the value of that commodity on which it is exercised, as every diminution must lower it. (Vol. I, p. 8.)

Ricardo goes on to reproach Smith:

1. With having "himself erected another standard measure of value" than labour. "Sometimes he speaks of corn, at other times of labour, as a standard measure; not the quantity of labour bestowed on the production of any object, but the quantity it can command in the market." (Vol. I, pp. 9 and 10.)

2. With having "admitted the principle without qualification and at the same time restricted its application to that early and rude state of society, which precedes both the accumulation of stock and the appropriation of land." (Vol. I, p. 21.)[10]

Ricardo sets out to prove that the ownership of land, that is, ground rent, cannot change the relative value of commodities and that the accumulation of capital has only a passing and fluctuating effect on the relative values determined by the comparative quantity of labour expended on their production. In support of this thesis, he gives his famous theory of ground rent, analyses capital, and ultimately finds nothing in it but accumulated labour. Then he develops a whole theory of wages and profits, and proves that wages and profits rise and fall in inverse ratio to each other, without affecting the relative value of the product. He does not neglect the influence that the accumulation of capital and its different aspects (fixed capital and circulating capital), as also the rate of wages, can have on the proportional value of products. In fact, they are the chief problems with which Ricardo is concerned.

Economy in the use of labour never fails to reduce the relative value* of a commodity, whether the saving be in the labour necessary to the manufac-

---

* Ricardo, as is well known, determines the value of a commodity by the quan-

ture of the commodity itself, or in that necessary to the formation of the capital, by the aid of which it is produced. (Vol. I, p. 28.) Under such circumstances the value of the deer, the produce of the hunter's day's labour, would be exactly equal to the value of the fish, the produce of the fisherman's day's labour. The comparative value of the fish and the game, would be entirely regulated by the quantity of labour realized in each; whatever might be the quantity of production, or however high or low general wages or profits might be. (Vol. I, p. 32.) In making labour the foundation of the value of commodities and the comparative quantity of labour which is necessary to their production, the rule which determines the respective quantities of goods which shall be given in exchange for each other, we must not be supposed to deny the accidental and temporary deviations of the actual or market price of commodities from this, their primary and natural price. (Vol. I, p. 105, *l. c.*) It is the cost of production which must ultimately regulate the price of commodities, and not, as has been often said, the proportion between supply and demand. (Vol. II, p. 253.)

Lord Lauderdale had developed the variations of exchange value according to the law of supply and demand, or of scarcity and abundance relatively to demand. In his opinion the value of a thing can increase when its quantity decreases or when the demand for it increases; it can decrease owing to an increase of its quantity or owing to the decrease in demand. Thus the value of a thing can change through eight different causes, namely, four causes that apply to the thing itself, and four causes that apply to money or to any other commodity which serves as a measure of its value. Here is Ricardo's refutation:

Commodities which *are monopolized,* either by an individual, or by a company, vary according to the law which Lord Lauderdale has laid down: they fall in proportion as the sellers augment their quantity, and rise in proportion to the eagerness of the buyers to purchase them; their price has no necessary connexion with their natural value: but the prices of commodities, which are subject to competition, and whose quantity may be increased in any moderate degree, will ultimately depend, not on the state of demand and supply, but on the increased or diminished cost of their production. (Vol. II, p. 259.)

We shall leave it to the reader to make the comparison between this simple, clear, precise language of Ricardo's and M. Proudhon's rhetorical attempts to arrive at the determination of relative value by labour time.

tity of labour necessary for its production. Owing, however, to the prevailing form of exchange in every mode of production based on production of commodities, including therefore the capitalist mode of production, this value is not expressed directly in quantities of labour but in quantities of some other commodity. The value of a commodity expressed in a quantity of some other commodity (whether money or not) is termed by Ricardo its relative value. *[Note by F. Engels to the German edition, 1885.]*

Ricardo shows us the real movement of bourgeois production, which constitutes value. M. Proudhon, leaving this real movement out of account, "fumes and frets" in order to invent new processes and to achieve the reorganization of the world on a would-be new formula, which formula is no more than the theoretical expression of the real movement which exists and which is so well described by Ricardo. Ricardo takes his starting point from present-day society to demonstrate to us how it constitutes value—M. Proudhon takes constituted value as his starting point to construct a new social world with the aid of this value. For him, M. Proudhon, constituted value must move around and become once more the constituting factor in a world already completely constituted according to this mode of evaluation. The determination of value by labour time, is, for Ricardo, the law of exchange value; for M. Proudhon, it is the synthesis of use value and exchange value. Ricardo's theory of values is the scientific interpretation of actual economic life; M. Proudhon's theory of values is the utopian interpretation of Ricardo's theory. Ricardo establishes the truth of his formula by deriving it from all economic relations, and by explaining in this way all phenomena, even those like ground rent, accumulation of capital and the relation of wages to profits, which at first sight seem to contradict it; it is precisely that which makes his doctrine a scientific system M. Proudhon, who has rediscovered this formula of Ricardo's by means of quite arbitrary hypotheses, is forced thereafter to seek out isolated economic facts which he twists and falsifies to pass them off as examples, already existing applications, beginnings of realization of his regenerating idea. (See our §3, *Application of Constituted Value* [pp. 58-75, this text].)

Now let us pass on to the conclusions M. Proudhon draws from value constituted (by labour time).

— A certain quantity of labour is equivalent to the product created by this same quantity of labour.

— Each day's labour is worth as much as another day's labour; that is to say, if the quantities are equal, one man's labour is worth as much as another man's labour: there is no qualitative difference. With the same quantity of work, one man's product can be given in exchange for another man's product. All men are wage workers getting equal pay for an equal time of work. Perfect equality rules the exchanges.

Are these conclusions the strict, natural consequences of value "constituted" or determined by labour time?

If the relative value of a commodity is determined by the quantity of labour required to produce it, it follows naturally that the relative value of labour, or wages, is likewise determined by the quantity of labour needed to produce the wages. Wages, that is, the relative value or the price of labour, are thus determined by the labour time needed to produce all that is necessary for the maintenance of the worker. *"Diminish the cost of production* of hats, and their price will ultimately fall to their new natural price, although the demand should be doubled, trebled, or quadrupled. *Diminish the cost of subsistence of men,* by diminishing the natural price of the food and clothing, by which life is sustained, and wages will ultimately fall, notwithstanding that the demand for labourers may very greatly increase." (Ricardo, Vol. II, p. 253.)

Doubtless, Ricardo's language is as cynical as can be. To put the cost of manufacture of hats and the cost of maintenance of men on the same plane is to turn men into hats. But do not make an outcry at the cynicism of it. The cynicism is in the facts and not in the words which express the facts. French writers like MM. Droz, Blanqui, Rossi and others take an innocent satisfaction in proving their superiority over the English economists, by seeking to observe the etiquette of a "humanitarian" phraseology; if they reproach Ricardo and his school for their cynical language, it is because it annoys them to see economic relations exposed in all their crudity, to see the mysteries of the bourgeoisie unmasked.

To sum up: Labour, being itself a commodity, is measured as such by the labour time needed to produce the labour-commodity. And what is needed to produce this labour-commodity? Just enough labour time to produce the objects indispensable to the constant maintenance of labour, that is, to keep the worker alive and in a condition to propagate his race. The natural price of labour is no other than the wage minimum.* If the current rate

---

* The thesis that the "natural," i.e., normal, price of labour power coincides with the wage minimum, i.e., with the equivalent in value of the means of subsistence absolutely indispensable for the life and procreation of the worker, was first put forward by me in *Sketches for a Critique of Political Economy (Deutsch-Französische Jahrbacher [Franco-German Annuals),* Paris 1844) and in *The Condition of the Working-Class in England in 1844.* As seen here, Marx at that time accepted the thesis. Lassalle took it over from both of us. Although, however, in reality wages have a constant tendency to approach the minimum, the above thesis is nevertheless incorrect. The fact that labour is regularly and on the average paid below its value cannot alter its value. In *Capital,* Marx has both put the above thesis right (Section on the Buying and Selling of Labour Power) and also (Chapter 25: *The General Law of Capitalist Accumulation)* analysed the circumstances which permit capitalist production to depress the price of labour power more and more below its value. *[Note by F. Engels to the German edition, 1885.]*

of wages rises above this natural price, it is precisely because the law of value put as a principle by M. Proudhon happens to be counterbalanced by the consequences of the varying relations of supply and demand. But the minimum wage is none the less the centre towards which the current rates of wages gravitate.

Thus relative value, measured by labour time, is inevitably the formula of the present enslavement of the worker, instead of being, as M. Proudhon would have it, the "revolutionary theory" of the emancipation of the proletariat.

Let us see now to what extent the application of labour time as a measure of value is incompatible with the existing class antagonism and the unequal distribution of the product between the immediate worker and the owner of accumulated labour.

Let us take a particular product, for example, linen. This product, as such, contains a definite quantity of labour. This quantity of labour will always be the same, whatever the reciprocal position of those who have collaborated to create this product.

Let us take another product: broadcloth, which has required the same quantity of labour as the linen.

If there is an exchange of these two products, there is an exchange of equal quantities of labour. In exchanging these equal quantities of labour time, one does not change the reciprocal position of the producers, any more than one changes anything in the situation of the workers and manufacturers among themselves. To say that this exchange of products measured by labour time results in an equality of payment for all the producers is to suppose that equality of participation in the product existed before the exchange. When the exchange of broadcloth for linen has been accomplished, the producers of broadcloth will share in the linen in a proportion equal to that in which they previously shared in the broadcloth.

M. Proudhon's illusion is brought about by his taking for a consequence what could be at most but a gratuitous supposition.

Let us go further.

Does labour time, as the measure of value, suppose at least that the days are *equivalent,* and that one man's day is worth as much as another's? No.

Let us suppose for a moment that a jeweller's day is equivalent to three days of a weaver; the fact remains that any change in the value of jewels relative to that of woven materials, unless it be the transitory result of the fluctuations of supply and demand, must have as its cause a reduction or an increase in the labour time expended in the production of one or the other. If three working days of different workers be related to one another in the ratio of 1 : 2 : 3, then every change in the relative value of their products will be a change in this same proportion of 1 : 2 : 3. Thus values can be measured by labour time, in spite of the inequality of value of different working days; but to apply such a measure we must have a comparative scale of the different working days: it is competition that sets up this scale.

Is your hour's labour worth mine? That is a question which is decided by competition.

Competition, according to an American economist, determines how many days of simple labour are contained in one day's compound labour. Does not this reduction of days of compound labour to days of simple labour suppose that simple labour is itself taken as a measure of value? If the mere quantity of labour functions as a measure of value regardless of quality, it presupposes that simple labour has become the pivot of industry. It presupposes that labour has been equalized by the subordination of man to the machine or by the extreme division of labour; that men are effaced by their labour; that the pendulum of the clock has become as accurate a measure of the relative activity of two workers as it is of the speed of two locomotives. Therefore, we should not say that one man's hour is worth another man's hour, but rather that one man during an hour is worth just as much as another man during an hour. Time is everything, man is nothing; he is at the most, time's carcase. Quality no longer matters. Quantity alone decides everything; hour for hour, day for day; but this equalizing of labour is not by any means the work of M. Proudhon's eternal justice; it is purely and simply a fact of modern industry.

In the automatic workshop, one worker's labour is scarcely distinguishable in any way from another worker's labour: workers can only be distinguished one from another by the length of time they take for their work. Nevertheless, this quantitative difference becomes, from a certain point of view, qualitative, in that the time they take for their work depends partly on purely material causes, such as physical constitution, age and sex; partly on purely negative moral causes, such as patience, imperturbability, diligence. In short, if there is a difference of quality in the labour of different workers, it is at most a quality of the last kind, which is far from being a distinctive speciality. This is what the state of affairs in modern industry amounts to in the last analysis. It is upon this equality, already realized in automatic labour, that M. Proudhon wields his smoothing-plane of "equalization," which he means to establish universally in "time to come"!

All the "equalitarian" consequences which M. Proudhon deduces from Ricardo's doctrine are based on a fundamental error. He confounds the value of commodities measured by the quantity of labour embodied in them with the value of commodities measured by *the value of labour.* If these two ways of measuring the value of commodities were equivalent, it could be said indifferently that the relative value of any commodity is measured by the quantity of labour embodied in it; or that it is measured by the quantity of labour it can buy; or again that it is measured by the quantity of labour which can acquire it. But this is far from being so. The value of labour can no more serve as a measure of value than the value of any other commodity. A few examples will suffice to explain still better what we have just stated.

If a muid* of corn cost two days' labour instead of one, it would have twice its original value; but it would not set in operation double the quantity of labour, because it would contain no more nutritive matter than before. Thus the value of the corn, measured by the quantity of labour used to produce it, would have doubled; but measured either by the quantity of labour it can buy or by the quantity of labour with which it can be bought, it would be far from having doubled. On the other hand, if the same labour produced twice as many clothes as before, their relative value would fall by half; but, nevertheless, this double quantity of clothing would not thereby be reduced to disposing over only half the quantity of labour, nor could the same labour command the double quantity of clothing; for half the clothes would still go on rendering the worker the same service as before.

Thus it is going against economic facts to determine the relative value of commodities by the value of labour. It is moving in a vicious circle, it is to determine relative value by a relative value which itself needs to be determined.

It is beyond doubt that M. Proudhon confuses the two measures, measure by the labour time needed for the production of a commodity and measure by the value of the labour. "Any man's labour," he says, "can buy the value it represents." Thus, according to him, a certain quantity of labour embodied in a product is equivalent to the worker's payment, that is, to the value of la-

---

* An old French measure equivalent to 18 hectolitres.

bour. It is the same reasoning that makes him confuse cost of production with wages.

"What are wages? They are the cost price of corn, etc., the integral price of all things." Let us go still further. "Wages are the proportionality of the elements which compose wealth." What are wages? They are the value of labour.

Adam Smith takes as the measure of value, now the time of labour needed for the production of a commodity, now the value of labour. Ricardo exposes this error by showing clearly the disparity of these two ways of measuring. M. Proudhon goes one better than Adam Smith in error by identifying the two things which the latter had merely put in juxtaposition.

It is in order to find the proper proportion in which workers should share in the products, or, in other words, to determine the relative value of labour, that M. Proudhon seeks a measure for the relative value of commodities. To find out the measure for the relative value of commodities he can think of nothing better than to give as the equivalent of a certain quantity of labour the sum total of the products it has created, which is as good as supposing that the whole of society consists merely of workers who receive their own produce as wages. In the second place, he takes for granted the equivalence of the working days of different workers. In short, he seeks the measure of the relative value of commodities in order to arrive at equal payment for the workers, and he takes the equality of wages as an already established fact, in order to go off on the search for the relative value of commodities. What admirable dialectics!

> Say and the economists after him have observed that labour being itself subject to valuation, being a commodity like any other commodity, it is moving in a vicious circle to treat it as the principle and the determining cause of value. In so doing, these economists, if they will allow me to say so, show a prodigious carelessness. Labour is said to *have value* not as a commodity itself, but in view of the values which it is supposed potentially to contain. The value of labour is a figurative expression, an anticipation of the cause for the effect. It is a fiction of the same stamp as the *productivity of capital*. Labour produces, capital has value.... By a sort of ellipsis one speaks of the value of labour.... Labour like liberty... is a thing vague and indeterminate by nature, but defined qualitatively by its object, that is to say, it becomes a reality by the product. [I: 61]
>
> But is there any need to dwell on this? The moment the economist (read M. Proudhon) changes the name of things, *vera rerum vocabula* [the true names of things], he is implicitly confessing his impotence and proclaiming himself not privy to the cause. (Proudhon, I, 188.)

We have seen that M. Proudhon makes the value of labour the "determining cause" of the value of products to such an extent that for him *wages,* the official name for the "value of labour," form the integral price of all things: that is why Say's objection troubles him. In labour as a commodity, which is a grim reality, he sees nothing but a grammatical ellipsis. Thus the whole of existing society, founded on labour as a commodity, is henceforth founded on a poetic license, a figurative expression. If society wants to "eliminate all the drawbacks" that assail it, well, let it eliminate all the ill-sounding terms, change the language; and to this end it has only to apply to the Academy for a new edition of its dictionary. After all that we have just seen, it is easy for us to understand why M. Proudhon, in a work on political economy, has to enter upon long dissertations on etymology and other parts of grammar. Thus he is still learnedly discussing the antiquated derivation of servus* from servare.** These philological dissertations have a deep meaning, an esoteric meaning—they form an essential part of M. Proudhon's argument.

Labour [power],[11] inasmuch as it is bought and sold, is a commodity like any other commodity, and has, in consequence, an exchange value. But the value of labour, or labour as a commodity, produces as little as the value of wheat, or wheat as a commodity, serves as food.

Labour "is worth" more or less, according to whether food commodities are more or less dear, whether the supply and demand of hands exist to such or such a degree, etc., etc.

Labour is not a "vague thing"; it is always some definite labour, it is never labour in general that is bought and sold. It is not only labour that is qualitatively defined by the object; but also the object which is determined by the specific quality of labour.

Labour, in so far as it is bought and sold, is itself a commodity. Why is it bought? "Because of the values it is supposed potentially to contain." But if a certain thing is said to be a commodity, there is no longer any question as to the reason why it is bought, that is, as to the utility to be derived from it, the application to be made of it. It is a commodity as an object of traffic. All M. Proudhon's arguments are limited to this: labour is not bought as an immediate object of consumption. No, it is bought as an instrument of production, as a machine would be bought. As a commodity, labour has value and does not produce. M. Proudhon might just as well have said that there is no such thing as a

---

* A servant, slave.

** To preserve.

commodity, since every commodity is obtained merely for some utilitarian purpose, and never as a commodity in itself.

In measuring the value of commodities by labour, M. Proudhon vaguely glimpses the impossibility of excluding labour from this same measure, in so far as labour has a value, as labour is a commodity. He has a misgiving that it is turning the wage minimum into the natural and normal price of immediate labour, that it is accepting the existing state of society. So, to get away from this fatal consequence, he faces about and asserts that labour is not a commodity, that it cannot have value. He forgets that he himself. has taken the value of labour as a measure, he forgets that his whole system rests on labour as a commodity, on labour which is bartered, bought, sold, exchanged for produce, etc., on labour. in fact, which is an immediate source of income for the worker. He forgets everything.

To save his system, he consents to sacrifice its basis.

*Et propter vitam vivendi perdere causas!**

We now come to a new definition of *"constituted* value."

"Value is the *proportional relation* of the products which constitute wealth." [I: 62]

Let us note in the first place that the simple phrase "relative or exchange value" implies the idea of some relation in which products are exchanged reciprocally. By giving the name "proportional relation" to this relation, no change is made in the relative value, except in the expression. Neither the depreciation nor the enhancement of the value of a product destroys its quality of being in some "proportional relation" with the other products which constitute wealth.

Why then this new term, which introduces no new idea?

"Proportional relation" suggests many other economic relations, such as proportionality in production, the true proportion between supply and demand, etc., and M. Proudhon is thinking of all that when he formulates this didactic paraphrase of marketable value.

In the first place, the relative value of products being determined by the comparative amount of labour used in the production of each of them, proportional relations, applied to this special case, stand for the respective quota of products which can be manufactured in a given time, and which in consequence are given in exchange for one another.

* And for the sake of life to lose the reason for living. (Juvenal, *Satires*, VIII.)

Let us see what advantage M. Proudhon draws from this proportional relation.

Everyone knows that when supply and demand are evenly balanced, the relative value of any product is accurately determined by the quantity of labour embodied in it, that is to say, that this relative value expresses the proportional relation precisely in the sense we have just attached to it. M. Proudhon inverts the order of things. Begin, he says, by measuring the relative value of product by the quantity of labour embodied in it, and supply and demand will infallibly balance one another. Production will correspond to consumption, the product will always be exchangeable. Its current price will express exactly its true value. Instead of saying like everyone else: when the weather is fine, a lot of people are to be seen going out for a walk, M. Proudhon makes his people go out for a walk in order to be able to ensure them fine weather.

What M. Proudhon gives as the consequence of marketable value determined *a priori* by labour time could be justified only by a law couched more or less in the following terms:

Products will in future be exchanged in the exact ratio of the labour time they have cost. Whatever may be the proportion of supply to demand, the exchange of commodities will always be made as if they had been produced proportionately to the demand. Let M. Proudhon take it upon himself to formulate and lay down such a law, and we shall relieve him of the necessity of giving proofs. If, on the other hand, he insists on justifying his theory, not as a legislator, but as an economist, he will have to prove that the *time* needed to create a commodity indicates exactly the degree of its *utility* and marks its proportional relation to the demand, and in consequence, to the total amount of wealth. In this case, if a product is sold at a price equal to its cost of production, supply and demand will always be evenly balanced; for the cost of production is supposed to express the true relation between supply and demand.

Actually, M. Proudhon sets out to prove that the labour time needed to create a product indicates its true proportional relation to needs, so that the things whose production costs the least time are the most immediately useful, and so on, step by step. The mere production of a luxury object proves at once, according to this doctrine, that society has spare time which allows it to satisfy a need for luxury.

M. Proudhon finds the very proof of his thesis in the observation that the most useful things cost the least time to produce, that society always begins with the easiest industries and successively "starts on the production of objects which cost more labour time and which correspond to a higher order of needs." [I: 57]

M. Proudhon borrows from M. Dunoyer the example of extractive industry—fruit-gathering, pasturage, hunting, fishing, etc.—which is the simplest, the least costly of industries, and the one by which man began "the first day of his second creation." The first day of his first creation is recorded in Genesis, which shows us God as the world's first manufacturer.

Things happen in quite a different way from what M. Proudhon imagines. The very moment civilization begins, production begins to be founded on the antagonism of orders, estates, classes, and finally on the antagonism of accumulated labour and actual labour. No antagonism, no progress. This is the law that civilization has followed up to our days. Till now the productive forces have been developed by virtue of this system of class antagonisms. To say now that, because all the needs of all the workers were satisfied, men could devote themselves to the creation of products of a higher order-to more complicated industries-would be to leave class antagonism out of account and turn all historical development upside down. It is like saying that because, under the Roman emperors, muræna were fattened in artificial fishponds, therefore there was enough to feed abundantly the whole Roman population. Actually, on the contrary, the Roman people had not enough to buy bread with, while the Roman aristocrats had slaves—enough to throw as fodder to the muræna.

The price of food has almost continuously risen, while the price of manufactured and luxury goods has almost continuously fallen. Take the agricultural industry itself: the most indispensable objects, like corn, meat, etc., rise in price, while cotton, sugar, coffee, etc., fall in a surprising proportion. And even among comestibles proper, the luxury articles, like artichokes, asparagus, etc., are today relatively cheaper than foodstuffs of prime necessity. In our age, the superfluous is easier to produce than the necessary. Finally, at different historical epochs, the reciprocal price relations are not only different, but opposed to one another. In the whole of the Middle Ages, agricultural products were relatively cheaper than manufactured products; in modern times they are in inverse ratio. Does this means that the utility of agricultural products has diminished since the Middle Ages?

The use of products is determined by the social conditions in which the consumers find themselves placed, and these conditions themselves are based on class antagonism.

Cotton, potatoes and spirits are objects of the most common use. Potatoes have engendered scrofula; cotton has to a great extent driven out flax and wool, although wool and flax are, in many cases, of greater utility, if only from the point of view of hygiene; finally, spirits have got the upper hand of beer and wine, although spirits used as an alimentary substance are everywhere recognized to be poison. For a whole century, governments struggled in vain against the European opium; economics prevailed, and dictated its orders to consumption.

Why are cotton, potatoes and spirits the pivots of bourgeois society? Because the least amount of labour is needed to produce them, and, consequently, they have the lowest price. Why does the minimum price determine the maximum consumption? Is it by any chance because of the absolute utility of these objects, their intrinsic utility, their utility insomuch as they correspond, in the most useful manner, to the needs of the worker as a man, and not to the man as a worker? No, it is because in a society founded on *poverty* the poorest products have the fatal prerogative of being used by the greatest number.

To say now that because the least costly things are in greater use, they must be of greater utility, is saying that the wide use of spirits, because of their low cost of production, is the most conclusive proof of their utility; it is telling the proletarian that potatoes are more wholesome for him than meat; it is accepting the present state of affairs; it is, in short, making an apology, with M. Proudhon, for a society without understanding it. In a future society, in which class antagonism will have ceased, in which there will no longer be any classes, use will no longer be determined by the *min*imum time of production; but the time of production devoted to different articles will be determined by the degree of their social utility.

To return to M. Proudhon's thesis; the moment the labour time necessary for the production of an article ceases to be the expression of its degree of utility, the exchange value of this same article, determined beforehand by the labour time embodied in it, becomes quite unable to regulate the true relation of supply to demand, that is, the proportional relation in the sense M. Proudhon at the moment attributes to it.

It is not the sale of a given product at the price of its cost of production that constitutes the "proportional relation" of supply to demand, or the proportional quota of this product relatively to the sum total of production; it is the *variations in supply and demand* that show the producer what amount of a given commodity he must produce in order to receive in exchange at least the cost of production. And as these variations are continually occurring, there is also a continual movement of withdrawal and application of capital in the different branches of industry.

> It is only in consequence of such variations that capital is *apportioned* precisely, in the requisite abundance and no more, to the production of the different commodities which happen to be in demand. With the rise or fall of price, profits are elevated above, or depressed below their general level, and capital is either encouraged to enter into, or is warned to depart from, the particular employment in which the variation has taken place.—— When we look to the markets of a large town, and observe how regularly they are supplied both with home and foreign commodities, in the quantity in which they are required, under all the circumstances of varying demand, arising from the caprice of taste, or a change in the amount of population, without often producing either the effects of a glut from a too abundant supply, or an enormously high price from the supply being unequal to the demand, we must confess that the principle which apportions capital to each trade *in the precise amount that is required,* is more active than is generally supposed. (Ricardo, Vol. I, pp. 105 and 108.)

If M. Proudhon admits that the value of products is determined by labour time, he should equally admit that it is the fluctuating movement alone that in society founded on individual exchanges makes labour the measure of value. There is no ready-made constituted "proportional relation," but only a constituting movement.

We have just seen in what sense it is correct to speak of "proportion" as of a consequence of value determined by labour time. We shall see now how this measure by time, called by M. Proudhon the "law of proportion," becomes transformed into a law of *disproportion.*

Every new invention that enables the production in one hour of that which has hitherto been produced in two hours depreciates all similar products on the market. Competition forces the producer to sell the product of two hours as cheaply as the product of one hour. Competition carries into effect the law according to which the relative value of a product is determined by the labour time needed to produce it. Labour time serving as the measure of marketable value becomes in this way the law of the continual *depreciation* of labour. We will say more. There will be depreciation not only of the commodities brought into the market, but also. of the instruments of production and of whole plants. This fact was already pointed out by Ricardo when he said: "By constantly increasing the facility of production, we constantly diminish the value of some of the commodities before produced." (Vol. II p. 59). Sismondi goes further. He sees in this "value *constituted*" by labour time, the source of all the contradictions of modern industry and commerce. He says:

> Mercantile value is always determined in the long run by the quantity of labour needed to obtain the thing evaluated: it is not what it has actually cost, but what it would cost in future with, perhaps, perfected means; and this quantity, although difficult to evaluate, is always faithfully established by competition.... It is on this basis that the demand of the seller as well as the supply of the buyer is reckoned. The former will perhaps declare that the thing has cost him ten days' labour; but if the latter realizes that it can henceforth be produced with eight days' labour, in the event of competition proving this to the two contracting parties, the value will be reduced, and the market price fixed at eight days only. Of course, each of the parties believes that the thing is useful, that it is desired, that without desire there would be no sale; but the fixing of the price has nothing to do with utility. (*Etudes*, etc., Vol. II, p. 267, Brussels edition.)

It is important to emphasize the point that what determines value is not the time taken to produce a thing, but the *minimum* time it could possibly be produced in, and this minimum is ascertained by competition. Suppose for a moment that there is no more competition and consequently no longer any means to ascertain the minimum of labour necessary for the production of a commodity; what will happen? It will suffice to spend six hours' work on the production of an object, in order to have the right, according to M. Proudhon, to demand in exchange six times as much as the one who has taken only one hour to produce the same object.

Instead of a "proportional relation," we have a disproportional relation, at any rate if we insist on sticking to relations, good or bad.

The continual depreciation of labour is only one side, one consequence of the evaluation of commodities by labour time. The excessive raising of prices, overproduction and many other features of industrial anarchy have their explanation in this mode of evaluation.

But does labour time used as a measure of value give rise at least to the proportional variety of products that so delights M. Proudhon?

On the contrary, monopoly in all its monotony follows in its wake and invades the world of products, just as to everybody's knowledge monopoly invades the world of the instruments of production. It is only in a few branches of industry, like the cotton industry, that very rapid progress can be made. The natural consequence of this progress is that the products of cotton manufacture, for instance, fall rapidly in price: but as the price of cotton goes down, the price of flax must go up in comparison. What will be the outcome? Flax will be replaced by cotton. In this way, flax has been driven out of almost the whole of North America. And we have obtained, instead of the proportional variety of products, the dominance of cotton.

What is left of this "proportional relation"? Nothing but the pious wish of an honest man who would like commodities to be produced in proportions which would permit of their being sold at an honest price. In all ages good-natured bourgeois and philanthropic economists have taken pleasure in expressing this innocent wish.

Let us hear what old *Boisguillebert* says:

> The price of commodities must always be *proportionate*; for it is such mutual understanding alone that can enable them to exist together *so as to give themselves to one another at any moment* (here is M. Proudhon's continual exchangeability) and reciprocally give birth to one another.... As wealth, then, is nothing but this continual intercourse between man and man, craft and craft, etc., it is a frightful blindness to go looking for the cause of misery elsewhere than in the cessation of such traffic brought about by a disturbance of proportion in prices. (*Dissertation sur la nature des richesses*, Daire's ed. [pp. 405, 408].)[12]

Let us listen also to a modern economist:

> The great law as necessary to be affixed to production, that is, the *law of proportion*, which alone can preserve the continuity of value.... The equivalent must be guaranteed.... All nations have attempted, at various periods of their history, by instituting numerous commercial regulations and restrictions, to effect, in some degree, the object here explained.... But the natural and inherent selfishness of man ... has urged him to break down all such regulations. Proportionate Production is the realization of the entire truth of the Science of Social Economy. (W. Atkinson, *Principles of Political Economy*, London 1840, pp. 170-195.)

Fuit Troja.[13] This correct proportion between supply and demand, which is beginning once more to be the object of so many wishes, ceased long ago to exist. It has passed into the stage of senility. It was possible only at a time when the means of production were limited, when the movement of exchange took place within very restricted bounds. With the birth of large-scale industry this correct proportion had to come to an end, and production is inevitably compelled to pass in continuous succession through vicissitudes of prosperity, depression, crisis, stagnation, renewed prosperity, and so on.

Those who, like Sismondi, wish to return to the correct proportion of production, while preserving the present basis of society, are reactionary, since, to be consistent, they must also wish to bring back all the other conditions of industry of former times.

What kept production in correct, or more or less correct, proportions? It was demand that dominated supply, that preceded it. Production followed close on the heels of consumption. Large-scale industry, forced by the very instruments at its disposal to produce on an ever-increasing scale, can no longer wait for demand. Production precedes consumption, supply compels demand.

In existing society, in industry based on individual exchange, anarchy of production, which is the source of so much misery, is at the same time the source of all progress.

Thus, one or the other:

Either you want the true proportions of past centuries with present-day means of production, in which case you are both reactionary and utopian.

Or you want progress without anarchy: in which case in order to preserve the productive forces, you must abandon individual exchange.

Individual exchange is consistent only with the small-scale industry of past centuries and its corollary of "correct proportion," or else with large-scale industry with all its train of misery and anarchy.

After all, the determination of value by labour time—the formula M. Proudhon gives us as the regenerating formula of the future—is therefore merely the scientific expression of the economic relations of present-day society, as was clearly and precisely demonstrated by Ricardo long before M. Proudhon.

But does the "equalitarian" application of this formula at least belong to M. Proudhon? Was he the first to think of reforming society by transforming all men into actual workers exchanging equal amounts of labour? Is it really for him to reproach the Communists—these people devoid of all knowledge of political economy, these "obstinately foolish men," these "paradise dreamers"—with not having found, before him, this "solution of the problem of the proletariat"?

Anyone who is in any way familiar with the trend of political economy in England cannot fail to know that almost all the Socialists in that country have, at different periods, proposed the equalitarian application of the Ricardian theory. We could quote for M. Proudhon: Hodgskin, *Political Economy,* 1827[14]; William Thompson, *An Inquiry into the Principles of the Distribution of Wealth Most Conducive to Human Happiness,* 1824; T. R. Edmonds, *Practical Moral and Political Economy,* 1828,* etc., etc., and four pages more of *etc.* We shall content ourselves with listening to an English *Communist,* Mr.[J. F.] Bray. We shall give the

* Published in London.

decisive passages in his remarkable work, *Labour's Wrongs and Labour's Remedy,* Leeds 1839, and we shall dwell some time upon it, firstly, because Mr. Bray is still little known in France, and secondly, because we think that we have discovered in him the key to the past, present and future works of M. Proudhon.

The only way to arrive at truth is to go at once to First Principles.... Let us ... go at once to the source from whence governments themselves have arisen.... By thus going to the origin of the thing, we shall find that every form of government, and every social and governmental wrong, owes its rise to the existing social system—to *the institution of property as it at present exists*—and that, therefore, if we would end our wrongs and our miseries at once and for ever, *the present arrangements of society must be totally subverted....* By thus fighting them upon their own ground, and with their own weapons, we shall avoid that senseless clatter respecting *"visionaries" and "theorists,"* with which they are so ready to assail all who dare move one step from that beaten track which "by authority," has been pronounced to be the right one. Before the conclusions arrived at by such a course of proceeding can be overthrown, the economists must unsay or disprove those established truths and principles on which their own arguments are founded. (Bray, pp. 17 and 41.)

It is *labour alone which bestows value....* Every man has an undoubted right to all that his honest labour can procure him. When he thus appropriates the *fruits of his labour,* he commits no injustice upon any other human being; for he interferes with no other man's right of doing the same with the produce of *his labour....* All these ideas of superior and inferior—of master and man—may be traced to the neglect of First Principles, and to the consequent rise of *inequality* of possessions; and such ideas will never be eradicated, nor the institutions founded upon them be subverted, so long as this inequality is maintained. Men have hitherto blindly hoped to remedy the present unnatural state of things destroying *existing inequality,* and leaving untouched the *cause* of the inequality; but it will shortly be seen ... that misgovernment is not a cause, but a consequence—that it is not the creator, but the created—*that it is the offspring of inequality of possessions;* and that the inequality of possessions is inseparably connected with our present social system. (Bray, pp. 33, 36 and 37).

Not only are the greatest advantages, but strict justice also, on the side of a system of equality.... Every man is a link, and an indispensable link, in the chain of effects—the beginning of which is but an idea, and the end, perhaps, the production of a piece of cloth. Thus, although we may entertain different feelings towards the several parties, it does not follow that one should be better paid for his labour than another. The inventor will ever receive, in addition to his just pecuniary reward, that which genius only can obtain from us-the tribute of our admiration....

From the very nature of labour and exchange, strict justice not only requires that all exchangers should be *mutually,* but that they should likewise be *equally,* benefited. Men have only two things which they can exchange with each other, namely, labour, and the produce of labour.... If a just system of exchanges were acted upon, the value of all articles would be determined by *the entire cost of production; and equal values should always exchange for equal values.* If, for instance, it take a hatter one day to make a hat, and a shoemaker the same time to make a pair of shoes—

supposing the material used by each to be of the same value—and they exchange these articles with each other, they are not only mutually but equally benefited: the advantage derived by either party cannot be a disadvantage to the other, as each has given the same amount of labour, and the materials made use of by each were of equal value. But if the hatter should obtain two pair of shoes for one hat—time and value of material being as before—the exchange would clearly be an unjust one. The hatter would defraud the shoemaker of one day's labour; and were the former to act thus in all his exchanges, he would receive, for the labour of *half a year,* the product of some other person's *whole year.* We have heretofore acted upon no other than this most unjust system of exchanges—the *workmen have given* the capitalist the labour of a whole year, in exchange for the value of only half a year—and from this, and not from the assumed inequality of bodily and mental powers in individuals, has arisen the inequality of wealth and power which at present exists around us. It is an inevitable condition of inequality of exchanges—of buying at one price and selling at another—that capitalists shall continue to be capitalists, and working men to be working men—the one a class of tyrants and the other a class of slaves—to eternity.... The whole transaction, therefore, plainly shows that the capitalists and proprietors do no more than give the working man, for his labour of one week, a part of the wealth which they obtained from him the week before!—which just amounts to giving him *nothing for something....* The whole transaction, therefore, between the producer and the capitalist is a palpable deception, a mere farce: it is, in fact, in thousands of instances, no other than a barefaced though legalized robbery. (Bray, pp. 45, 48, 49 and 50).

... the gain of the employer will never cease to be the loss of the employed—until the exchanges between the parties are equal; and exchanges never can be equal while society is divided into capitalists and producers—the last living upon their labour and the first bloating upon the profit of that labour.

It is plain [continues Mr. Bray] that, establish whatever form of government we will ... we may talk of morality and brotherly love ... no reciprocity can exist where there are unequal exchanges. Inequality of exchanges, as being the cause of inequality of possessions, is the secret enemy that devours us. (Bray, pp. 51 and 52.)

It has been deduced, also, from a consideration of the intention and end of society, not only that all men should labour, and thereby become exchangers, but that equal values should always exchange for equal values —and that, as the gain of one man ought never to be the loss of another, value should ever be determined by cost of production. But we have seen, that, under the present arrangements of society ... the gain of the capitalist and the rich man is always the loss of the workman—that this result will invariably take place, and the poor man be left entirely at the mercy of the rich man, under any and every form of government, so long as there is inequality of exchanges—and that equality of exchanges can be insured only under social arrangements in which labour is universal.... If exchanges were equal, would the wealth of the present capitalists gradually go from them to the working classes. (Bray, pp. 53-55.)

So long as this system of unequal exchanges is tolerated, the producers will be almost as poor and as ignorant and as hardworked as they are at present, *even if every governmental burthen be swept away and* all *taxes be abolished* ... nothing but a total change of system—an equality of labour and exchanges—can alter this state of rights.... The producers have but to make an effort—and by them must every effort for their own redemption be made—and their chains will be snapped asunder for ever.... As an end, the political equality is there a failure, as a means, also, it is there a failure.

Where equal exchanges are maintained, the gain of one man cannot be the loss of another; for every exchange is then simply a *transfer,* and not a sacrifice, of labour and wealth. Thus, although under a social system based on equal exchanges, a parsimonious man may become rich, his wealth will be no more than the accumulated produce of his own labour. He may exchange his wealth, or he may give it to others ... but a rich man cannot continue wealthy for any length of time after he has ceased to labour. Under equality of exchanges, wealth cannot have, as it now has, a procreative and apparently self-generating power, such as replenishes all waste from consumption; for, unless it be renewed by labour, wealth, when once consumed, is given up for ever. That which is now called *profit* and *interest* cannot exist, as such in connection with equality of exchanges; for producer and distributor would be alike remunerated, and the sum total of their labour would determine the value of the article created and brought to the hands of the consumer....

The principle of equal exchanges, therefore, must from its very nature ensure *universal labour.* (Bray, pp. 67, 88, 89, 94, 109-110.)

After having refuted the objections of the economists *to communism,* Mr. Bray goes on to say:

If, then, a changed character be essential to the success of the social system of community in its most perfect form—and if, likewise, the present system affords no circumstances and no facilities for effecting the requisite change of character and preparing man for the higher and better state desired—it is evident that these things must necessarily remain as they are, ... or else some preparatory step must be discovered and made use of—some movement partaking partly of the present and partly of the desired system—some intermediate resting-place, to which society may go with all its faults and its follies, and from which it may move forward, imbued with those qualities and attributes without which the system of community and equality cannot as such have existence. (Bray, p. 134.)

The whole movement would require only co-operation in its simplest form.... Cost of production would in every instance determine value; and equal values would always exchange for equal values. If one person worked a whole week, and another worked only half a week, the first would receive double the remuneration of the last; but this extra pay of the one would not be at the expense of the other, nor would the loss incurred by the last man fall in any way upon the first. Each person would exchange the wages he individually received, for commodities of the same value as his respective wages; and in no case could the gain of one man or one trade be a loss to another man or another trade. The labour of every individual *would alone determine* his gains or his losses....

... By means of general and local boards of trade... the quantities of the various commodities required for consumption—the relative value of each in regard to each other—the number of hands required in various trades and descriptions of labour—and all other matters connected with production and distribution, could in a short time be as easily determined for a

nation as for an individual company under the present arrangements....
As individuals compose families, and families towns, under the existing
system, so likewise would they after the joint-stock change had been
effected. The present distribution of people in towns and villages, bad as
it is, would not be directly interfered with.... Under this joint-stock system, the same as under that now existing, every individual would be at
liberty to accumulate as much as he pleased, and to enjoy such accumula-
tions when and where he might think proper.... The great productive
section of the community ... is divided into an indefinite number of smaller
sections, all working, producing and exchanging their products on a footing
of the most perfect equality.... And the joint-stock modification (which is
nothing but a concession to present-day society in order to obtain communism), by being so constituted as to admit of *individual property in productions* in connection with a *common property in productive powers—making*
every individual dependent on his own exertions, and at the same time
allowing him an equal participation in every advantage afforded by nature
and art—is fitted to take society as it is, and to prepare the way for other
and better changes. (Bray, pp. 158, 160, 162, 168 and 194.)

We now only need to reply in a few words to Mr. Bray who
without us and in spite of us had managed to supplant M. Proudhon, except that Mr. Bray, far from claiming the last word on
behalf of humanity, proposes merely measures which he thinks
good for a period of transition between existing society and a
community regime.

One hour of Peter's labour exchanges for one hour of Paul's
labour. That is Mr. Bray's fundamental axiom.

Let us suppose Peter has twelve hours' labour before him, and
Paul only six. Peter will be able to make with Paul an exchange
of only six for six. Peter will consequently have six hours' labour
left over. What will he do with these six hours' labour?

Either he will do nothing—in which case he will have worked six
hours for nothing; or else he will remain idle for another six hours
to get even; or else, as a last resource, he will give these six hours'
labour, which he has no use for, to Paul into the bargain.

What in the end will Peter have earned more than Paul? Some
hours of labour? No! He will have gained only hours of leisure; he
will be forced to play the loafer for six hours. And in order that
this new right to loaf might be not only relished but sought after
in the new society, this society would have to find in idleness its
highest bliss, and to look upon labour as a heavy shackle from
which it must break free at all costs.

And indeed, to return to our example, if only these hours of
leisure that Peter has gained in excess of Paul were really a
gain! Not in the least. Paul, beginning by working only six hours,
attains by steady and regular work a result that Peter secures
only by beginning with an excess of work. Everyone will want to

be Paul, there will be a competition to occupy Paul's position, a competition in idleness.

Well, then! What has the exchange of equal quantities of labour brought us? Overproduction, depreciation, excess of labour followed by unemployment; in short, economic relations such as we see in present-day society, minus the competition of labour.

No! We are wrong! There is still an expedient which may save this new society of Peters and Pauls. Peter will consume by himself the product of the six hours' labour which he has left. But from the moment he has no longer to exchange because he has produced, he has no need to produce for exchange; and the whole hypothesis of a society founded on the exchange and division of labour will fall to the ground. Equality of exchange will have been saved by the simple fact that exchange will have ceased to be: Paul and Peter would arrive at the position of Robinson.

Thus, if all the members of society are supposed to be immediate workers, the exchange of equal quantities of hours of labour is possible only on condition that the number of hours to be spent on material production is agreed on beforehand. But such an agreement negates individual exchange.

We still come to the same result, if we take as our starting point not the distribution of the products created but the act of production. In large-scale industry, Peter is not free to fix for himself the time of his labour, for Peter's labour is nothing without the co-operation of all the Peters and all the Pauls who make up the workshop. This explains very well the dogged resistance which the English factory owners put up to the Ten Hours' Bill. They knew only too well that a two-hours' reduction of labour granted to women and children[15] would carry with it an equal reduction of working hours for adult men. It is in the nature of large-scale industry that working hours should be equal for all. What is today the result of capital and the competition of workers among themselves will be tomorrow, if you sever the relation between labour and capital, an actual agreement based upon the relation between the sum of productive forces and the sum of existing needs.

But such an agreement is a condemnation of individual exchange, and we are back again at our first conclusion!

In principle, there is no exchange of products-but there is the exchange of the labour which co-operated in production. The mode of exchange of products depends upon the mode of exchange of the productive forces. In general, the form of exchange of products corresponds to the form of production. Change the latter, and the former will change in consequence. Thus in the history of society we see that the mode of exchanging products is regulated by the mode of producing them. Individual exchange corresponds also to a definite mode of production which itself corresponds to class antagonism. There is thus no individual exchange without the antagonism of classes.

But the honest conscience refuses to see this obvious fact. So long as one is a bourgeois, one cannot but see in this relation of antagonism a relation of harmony and eternal justice, which allows no one to gain at the expense of another. For the bourgeois, individual exchange can exist without any antagonism of classes. For him, these are two quite unconnected things. Individual exchange, as the bourgeois conceives it, is far from resembling individual exchange as it actually exists in practice.

Mr. Bray turns the *illusion* of the respectable bourgeois into an *ideal* he would like to attain. In a purified individual exchange, freed from all the elements of antagonism he finds in it, he sees an *"equalitarian"* relation which he would like society to adopt generally.

Mr. Bray does not see that this equalitarian relation, *this corrective ideal* that he would like to apply to the world, is itself nothing but the reflection of the actual world; and that therefore it is totally impossible to reconstitute society on the basis of what is merely an embellished shadow of it. In proportion as this shadow takes on substance again, we perceive that this substance, far from being the transfiguration dreamt of, is the actual body of existing society.*

§3. APPLICATION OF THE LAW OF THE PROPORTIONALITY OF VALUE

A) Money

"Gold and silver were the first commodities to have their value constituted." [I: 69]

---

* Mr. Bray's theory, like all theories, has found supporters who have allowed themselves to be deluded by appearances. *Equitable-labour-exchange bazaars* have been set up in London, Sheffield, Leeds and many other towns in England. These bazaars have all ended in scandalous failures after having absorbed considerable capital. The taste for them has gone for ever. You are warned, Mr. Proudhon! *[Note by Marx.]* It is known that Proudhon did not take this warning to heart. In 1849 he himself made an attempt with a new Exchange Bank in Paris. The bank, however, failed before it had got going properly: a court case against Proudhon had to serve to cover its collapse. *[Note by F. Engels to the German edition, 1885.]*

Thus gold and silver are the first applications of "value constituted" ... by M. Proudhon. And as M. Proudhon constitutes the value of products determining it by the comparative amount of labour embodied in them, the only thing he had to do was to prove that *variations* in the value of gold and silver are always explained by variations in the labour time taken to produce them. M. Proudhon has no intention of doing so. He speaks of gold and silver not as commodities, but as money.

His only logic, if logic it be, consists in juggling with the capacity of gold and silver to be used as *money* for the benefit of all the commodities which have the property of being evaluated by labour time. Decidedly there is more naiveté than malice in this jugglery.

A useful product, once it has been evaluated by the labour time needed to produce it, is always acceptable in exchange; witness, cries M. Proudhon, gold and silver, which exist in my desired conditions of "exchangeability"! Gold and silver, then, are value which has reached a state of constitution: they are the incorporation of M. Proudhon's idea. He could not have been happier in his choice of an example. Gold and silver, apart from their capacity of being commodities, evaluated like other commodities, in labour time, have also the capacity of being the universal agents of exchange, of being money. By now considering gold and silver as an application of *"value constituted"* by labour time, nothing is easier than to prove that all commodities whose value is constituted by labour time will always be exchangeable, will be money.

A very simple question occurs to M. Proudhon. Why have gold and silver the privilege of typifying "constituted value"?

> The special function which usage has devolved upon the precious metals, that of serving as a medium for trade, is purely conventional, and any other commodity could, less conveniently perhaps, but just as reliably, fulfil this function. Economists recognize this, and cite more than one example. What then is the reason for this universal preference for metals as money? And what is the explanation of this specialization of the functions of money—which has no analogy in political economy?... Is it possible to *reconstruct the series* from which *money* seems to have broken away, and hence to trace it back to its true principle? [I: 68-69]

By formulating the question in these terms, M. Proudhon has presupposed the existence of *money*. The first question he should have asked himself was, why, in exchanges as they are actually constituted, it has been necessary to individualize exchangeable value, so to speak, by the creation of a special agent of exchange. Money is not a thing, it is a social relation. Why is the money relation a production relation like any other economic relation, such as the division of labour, etc.? If M. Proudhon had properly taken account of this relation, he would not have seen in money an exception, an element detached from a series unknown or needing reconstruction.

He would have realized, on the contrary, that this relation is a link, and, as such, closely connected with a whole chain of other economic relations; that this relation corresponds to a definite mode of production neither more nor less than does individual exchange. What does *he* do? He starts off by detaching money from the actual mode of production as a whole, and then makes it the first member of an imaginary series, of a series to be reconstructed.

Once the necessity for a specific agency of exchange, that is, for money, has been recognized, all that remains to be explained is why this particular function has devolved upon gold and silver rather than upon any other commodity. This is a secondary question, which is explained not by the chain of production relations, but by the specific qualities inherent in gold and silver as substances. If all this has made economists for once "go outside the domains of their own science, to dabble in physics, mechanics, history and so on," as M. Proudhon reproaches them with doing, they have merely done what they were compelled to do. The question was no longer within the domain of political economy.

"What no economist," says M. Proudhon, "has either seen or understood is the *economic reason* which has determined, in favour of the precious metals, the favour they enjoy." [I: 69]

This economic reason which nobody—with good ground indeed—has seen or understood, M. Proudhon has seen, understood and bequeathed to posterity.

> What nobody else has noticed is that, of all commodities, gold and silver were the first to have their value attain constitution. In the patriarchal period, gold and silver were still bartered and exchanged in ingots but even then they showed a visible tendency to become dominant and received a marked preference. *Little by little* the sovereigns took possession of them and affixed their seal to them: and of this sovereign consecration was born money, that is, the commodity *par excellence*, which, notwithstanding all the shocks of commerce, retains a definite proportional value and makes itself accepted for all payments... The distinguishing characteristic of gold and silver is due, I repeat, to the fact that, thanks to their metallic properties, to the difficulties of their production, and above all to the intervention of state authority, they early won stability and authenticity as commodities.

To say that, of all commodities, gold and silver were the first to have their value constituted, is to say, after all that has gone before, that gold and silver were the first to attain the status of money. This is M. Proudhon's great revelation, this is the truth that none had discovered before him.

If, by these words, M. Proudhon means that of all commodities gold and silver are the ones whose time of production was known the earliest, this would be yet another of the suppositions with which he is so ready to regale his readers. If we wished to harp on this patriarchal erudition, we would inform M. Proudhon that it was the time needed to produce objects of prime necessity, such as iron, etc., which was the first to be known. We shall spare him Adam Smith's classic bow.[16]

But, after all that, how can M. Proudhon go on talking about the constitution of a value, since a value is never constituted by itself? It is constituted, not by the time needed to produce it by itself, but in relation to the quota of each and every other product which can be created in the same time. Thus the constitution of the value of gold and silver presupposes an already completed constitution of a number of other products.

It is then not the commodity that has attained, in gold and silver, the status of "constituted value," it is M. Proudhon's "constituted value" that has attained, in gold and silver, the status of money.

Let us now make a closer examination of these *economic reasons* which, according to M. Proudhon, have bestowed upon gold and silver the advantage of being raised to the status of money sooner than other products, thanks to their having passed through the constitutive phase of value.

These economic reasons are: the "visible tendency to become dominant," the "marked preference" even in the "patriarchal period," and other circumlocutions about the actual fact—which increase the difficulty, since they multiply the fact by multiplying the incidents which M. Proudhon brings in to explain the fact. M. Proudhon has not yet exhausted all the so-called economic reasons. Here is one of sovereign, irresistible force:

"Money is born of sovereign consecration: the sovereigns take possession of gold and silver and affix their seal to them." [I:69]

Thus the whim of sovereigns is for M. Proudhon the highest reason in political economy.

Truly, one must be destitute of all historical knowledge not to know that it is the sovereigns who in all ages have been subject to economic conditions, but they have never dictated laws to them. Legislation, whether political or civil, never does more than proclaim, express in words, the will of economic relations.

Was it the sovereign who took possession of gold and silver to make them the universal agents of exchange by affixing his seal to them? Or was it not, rather, these universal agents of exchange which took possession of the sovereign and forced him to affix his seal to then] and thus give them a political consecration?

The impress which was and is still given to money is not that of its value but of its weight. The stability and authenticity M. Proudhon speaks of apply only to the standard of the money; and this standard indicates how much metallic matter there is in a coined piece of money. "The sole intrinsic value of a silver mark," says Voltaire, with his habitual good sense, "is a mark of silver, half a pound weighing eight ounces. The weight and the standard alone form this intrinsic value." (Voltaire, *Système de Law*).[17] But the question: how much is an ounce of gold or silver worth, remains none the less. If a cashmere from the *Grand Colbert* stores bore the trade mark *pure wool*, this trade mark would not tell you the value of the cashmere. There would still remain the question: how much is wool worth? Says M. Proudhon:

> Philip I, King of France, mixes with Charlemagne's gold pound a third of alloy, imagining that, having the monopoly of the manufacture of money, he could do what is done by every tradesman who has the monopoly of a product. What was actually this debasement of the currency for which Philip and his successors have been so much blamed? It was perfectly sound reasoning from the point of view of commercial practice, but very unsound economic science, viz., to suppose that, as supply and demand regulate value, it is possible, either by producing an artificial scarcity or by monopolizing manufacture, to increase the estimation and consequently the value of things; and that this is true of gold and silver as of corn, wine, oil or tobacco. But Philip's fraud was no sooner suspected than his money was reduced to its true value, and he himself lost what he had thought to gain from his subjects. The same thing has happened as a result of every similar attempt. [I: 70-71]

It has been proved times without number that, if a prince takes into his head to debase the currency, it is he who loses. What he gains once at the first issue he loses every time the falsified coinage returns to him in the form of taxes, etc. But Philip and his successors were able to protect themselves more or less against this loss, for, once the debased coinage was put into circulation, they hastened to order a general re-minting of money on the old footing.

And besides, if Philip I had really reasoned like M. Proudhon, he would not have reasoned well "from the commercial point of view." Neither Philip I nor M. Proudhon displays any mercantile genius in imagining that it is possible to alter the value of gold as well as that of every other commodity merely because their value is determined by the relation between supply and demand.

If King Philip had decreed that one muid of wheat was in future to be called two muids of wheat, he would have been a swindler. He would have deceived all *the rentiers,* all the people who were entitled to receive a hundred muids of wheat. He would have been the cause of all these people receiving only fifty instead of a hundred. Suppose the king owed a hundred muids of wheat; he would have had to pay only fifty. But in commerce a hundred such muids would never have been worth more than fifty. By changing the name we do not change the thing. The quantity of wheat, whether supplied or demanded, will be neither decreased nor increased by this mere change of name. Thus, the relation between supply and demand being just the same in spite of this change of name, the price of wheat will undergo no real change. When we speak of the supply and demand of things, we do not speak of the supply and demand of the name of things. Philip I was not a maker of gold or silver, as M. Proudhon says; he was a maker of names for coins. Pass off your French cashmeres as Asiatic cashmeres, and you may deceive a buyer or two; but once the fraud becomes known, your so-called Asiatic cashmeres will drop to the price of French cashmeres. When he put a false label on gold and silver, King Philip could deceive only so long as the fraud was not known. Like any other shopkeeper, he deceived his customers by a false. description of his wares, which could not last for long. He was bound sooner or later to suffer the rigour of commercial laws. Is this what M. Proudhon wanted to prove? No. According to him, it is from the sovereign and not from commerce that money gets its value. And what has he really proved? That commerce is more sovereign than the sovereign. Let the sovereign decree that one mark shall in future be two marks, commerce will keep on saying that these two marks are worth no more than one mark was formerly.

But, for all that, the question of value determined by the quantity of labour has not been advanced a step. It still remains to be decided whether the value of these two marks (which have become what one mark was once) is determined by the cost of production or by the law of supply and demand.

M. Proudhon continues:

> It should even be borne in mind that if, instead of debasing the currency, it had been in the king's power to double its bulk, the exchange value of gold and silver would immediately have dropped by half, always from reasons of proportion and equilibrium. [I: 71]

If this opinion, which M. Proudhon shares with the other economists, is valid, it argues in favour of the latter's doctrine of supply and demand, and in no way in favour of M. Proudhon's proportionality. For, whatever the quantity of labour embodied in the doubled bulk of gold and silver, its value would have dropped by half, the demand having remained the same and the supply having doubled. Or can it be, by any chance, that the "*law of proportionality*" would become confused this time with the so much disdained law of supply and demand? This true proportion of M. Proudhon's is indeed so elastic, is capable of so many variations, combinations and permutations, that it might well coincide for once with the relation between supply and demand.

To make "every commodity acceptable in exchange, if not in practice then at least by right," on the basis of the role of gold and silver is, then, to misunderstand this role. Gold and silver are acceptable by right only because they are acceptable in practice; and they are acceptable in practice because the present organization of production needs a universal medium of exchange. Right is only the official recognition of fact.

We have seen that the example of money as an application of value which has attained constitution was chosen by M. Proudhon only to smuggle through his whole doctrine of exchangeability, that is to say, to prove that every commodity assessed by its cost of production must attain the status of money. All this would be very fine, were it not for the awkward fact that precisely gold and silver, as money, are of all commodities the only ones not determined by their cost of production; and this is so true that in circulation they can be replaced by paper. So long as there is a certain proportion observed between the requirements of circulation and the amount of money issued, be it paper, gold, platinum or copper money, there can be no question of a proportion to be observed between the intrinsic value (cost of production) and the nominal value of money. Doubtless, in international trade, money is determined, like any other commodity, by labour time. But it is also true that gold and silver in international trade are means of exchange as products and not as money. In other words, they lose this characteristic of "stability and authenticity," of "sovereign consecration," which, for M. Proudhon, forms their specific characteristic. Ricardo understood this truth so well that, after basing his whole system on value determined by labour time, and after saying: "*Gold and silver,* like all other commodities, are valuable only in proportion to the quantity of labour necessary to produce them, and bring them to market," he adds, nevertheless, that the value of *money* is not

determined by the labour time its substance embodies, but by
the law of supply and demand only.

> Though it [paper money] has no intrinsic value, yet, by limiting its quan-
> tity, its value in exchange is as great as an equal denomination of coin, or
> of buiIion in that coin. On the same principle, too, namely, by limitation of
> its quantity, a debased coin would circulate at the value it should bear, if
> it were of the legal weight and fineness, and not at the value of the
> quantity of metal which it actually contained. In the history of the British
> coinage, we find, accordingly, that the currency was never depreciated in
> the same proportion that it was debased; the reason of which was, that it
> never was increased in quantity, in proportion to its diminished intrinsic
> value. (Ricardo, *loc. cit.* [pp. 206-207])

This is what J. B. Say observes on this passage of Ricardo's:

> This *example* should suffice, I think, to convince the author that the basis
> of all value is not the amount of labour needed to make a commodity, but
> the need felt for that commodity, balanced by its scarcity.[18]

Thus money, which for Ricardo is no longer a value determined by labour time, and which J. B. Say therefore takes as an
example to convince Ricardo that the other values could not be
determined by labour time either, this money, I say, taken by J.
B. Say as an example of a value determined exclusively by supply and demand, becomes for M. Proudhon the example *par ex-
cellence of* the application of value constituted ... by labour time.

To conclude, if money is not a value "constituted" by labour
time, it is all the less likely that it could have anything in common with M. Proudhon's true "proportion." Gold and silver are
always exchangeable, because they have the special function of
serving as the universal agent of exchange, and in no wise because they exist in a quantity proportional to the sum total of
wealth; or, to put it still better, they are always proportional
because, alone of all commodities, they serve as money, the universal agent of exchange, whatever their quantity in relation to
the sum total of wealth. "A circulation can never be so abundant
as to overflow; for by diminishing its value, in the same proportion you will increase its quantity, and by increasing its value,
diminish its quantity." (Ricardo [II: 205])

"What an imbroglio this political economy is!" cries M. Proudhon. [I: 72]

"'Cursed gold!' cries a Communist flippantly" (through the
mouth of M. Proudhon). "You might as well say: Cursed wheat,
cursed vines, cursed sheep!—for just like gold and silver, *every
commercial value* must attain its strict and exact determination."
[I: 73]

The idea of making sheep and vines attain the status of money is not new. In France, it belongs to the age of Louis XIV. At that period, money having begun to establish its omnipotence, the depreciation of all other commodities was being complained of, and the time when "every commercial value" might attain its strictly, exact determination, the status of money, was being eagerly invoked. Even in the writings of Boisguillebert, one of the oldest of French economists, we find: "Money then, by the arrival of innumerable competitors in the form of commodities themselves, re-established in their true values, will be thrust back again within its natural limits." *(Economistes financiers du dix-huitième siècle*, Daire edition, p. 422.)

One sees that the first illusions of the bourgeoisie are also their last.

B) Surplus Labour

"In works on political economy we read this absurd hypothesis: *If the price of everything were doubled....* As if the price of everything were not the proportion of things—and one could double a proportion, a relation, a law!" (Proudhon, Vol. I, p. 81.)

Economists have fallen into this error through not knowing how to apply the "law of proportionality" and of "constituted value."

Unfortunately in the very same work by M. Proudhon, Volume 1, p. 110, we read the absurd hypothesis that, "if wages rose generally, the price of everything would rise." Furthermore, if we find the phrase in question in works on political economy, we also find an explanation of it. "When one speaks of the price of all commodities going up or down, one always excludes some one commodity. The excluded commodity is, in general, money or labour." *(Encyclopaedia Metropolitana or Universal Dictionary of Knowledge*, Vol. IV, Article *Political Economy*, by Senior,* London 1836. Regarding the phrase under discussion, see also J. St. Mill: *Essays on Some Unsettled Questions of Political Economy*, London 1844, and Tooke: *A History of Prices, etc.*, London 1838.[19])

Let us pass now to the *second application* of "constituted value," and of other proportions-whose only defect is their lack of proportion. And let us see whether M. Proudhon is happier here than in the *monetization* of sheep.

An axiom generally admitted by economists is that all labour must leave a surplus. In my opinion this proposition is universally and absolutely true:

---

* N. W. Senior

it is the corollary of the law of proportion, which may be regarded as the summary of the whole of economic science. But, if the economists will permit me to say so, the principle that all *labour must leave a surplus* is meaningless according to their theory, and is not susceptible of any *demonstration*. (Proudhon [I: 73].)

To prove that all labour must leave a surplus, M. Proudhon personifies society; he turns it into a *person-society—a* society which is not by any means a society of persons, since it has its laws apart, which have nothing in common with the persons of which society is composed, and its "own intelligence," which is not the intelligence of common men, but an intelligence devoid of common sense. M. Proudhon reproaches the economists with not having understood the personality of this collective being. We have pleasure in confronting him with the following passage from an American economist, who accuses the economists of just the opposite:

> The moral entity—the grammatical being called a nation, has been clothed in attributes that have no real existence except in the imagination of those who metamorphose a word into a thing.... This has given rise to many difficulties and to some deplorable misunderstandings in political economy. (Th. Cooper, *Lectures on the Elements of Political Economy,* Columbia, 1826.[20])

"This principle of surplus labour," continues M. Proudhon, "is true of individuals only because it emanates from society, which thus confers on them the benefit of its own laws." [I: 75] Does M. Proudhon mean thereby merely that the production of the social individual exceeds that of the isolated individual? Is M. Proudhon referring to this excess of the production of associated individuals over that of non-associated individuals? If so, we could quote for him a hundred economists who have expressed this simple truth without any of the mysticism with which M. Proudhon surrounds himself. This, for example, is what Mr. Sadler says:

> Combined labour produces results which individual exertion could never accomplish. As mankind, therefore, multiply in number, the products of their united industry would greatly exceed the amount of any mere arithmetical addition calculated on such an increase. in the mechanical arts, as well as in pursuits of science, a man may achieve more in a day ... than a solitary ... individual could perform in his whole life.... Geometry says ... that the whole is only equal to the sum of all its parts; as applied to the subject before us, this axiom would be false. Regarding labour, the great pillar of human existence, it may be said that the entire product of combined exertion almost infinitely exceeds all which individual and disconnected efforts could possibly accomplish. (T. Sadler, *The Law of Population,* London 1830.[21])

To return to M. Proudhon. Surplus labour, he says, is explained by the person-society. The life of this person is guided by laws, the opposite of those which govern the activities of man as an individual. He desires to prove this by *"facts."*

The discovery of an economic process can never provide the inventor with a profit equal to that which he procures for society.... It has been remarked that railway enterprises are much less a source of wealth for the contractors than for the state.... The average cost of transporting commodities by road is 18 centimes per ton per kilometre, from the collection of the goods to their delivery. It has been calculated that at this rate an ordinary railway enterprise would not obtain 10 per cent net profit, a result approximately equal to that of a road-transport enterprise. But let us suppose that the speed of rail transport compared with that of road transport is as 4 is to 1. Since in society time is value itself, the railway would, prices being equal, present an advantage of 400 per cent over road transport. Yet this enormous advantage, very real for society, is far from being realized in the same proportion for the carrier, who, while bestowing upon society an extra value of 400 per cent does not for his own part draw 10 per cent. To bring the matter home still more pointedly, let us suppose, in fact, that the railway puts up its rate to 25 centimes, the cost of road transport remaining at 18: it would instantly lose all its consignments. Senders, receivers, everybody would return to the van, to the primitive waggon if necessary. The locomotive would be abandoned. A social advantage of 400 per cent would be sacrificed to a private loss of 35 per cent. The reason for this is easily grasped: the advantage resulting from the speed of the railway is entirely social, and each individual participates in it only in a minute proportion (it must be remembered that at the moment we are dealing only with the transport of goods), while the loss strikes the consumer directly and personally. A social profit equal to 400 represents for the individual, if society is composed only of a million men, four ten-thousandths; while a loss of 33 per cent for the consumer would suppose a social deficit of 33 millions. (Proudhon [I: 75, 76].)

We may even overlook the fact that M. Proudhon expresses a quadrupled speed as 400 per cent of the original speed; but that he should bring into relation the percentage of speed and the percentage of profit and establish a proportion between two relations which, although measured separately by percentages, are nevertheless incommensurable with each other, is to establish a proportion between the percentages without reference to denominations.

Percentages are always percentages, 10 per cent and 400 per cent are commensurable; they are to each other as 10 is to 400. Therefore, concludes M. Proudhon, a profit of 10 per cent is worth forty times less than a quadrupled speed. To save appearances, he says that, for society, time is money. This error arises from his recollecting vaguely that there is a connection between value and labour time, and he hastens to identify labour time with transport time; that is, he identifies the few firemen, drivers and others, whose labour time is actually transport time, with the whole of society. Thus at one blow, speed has become capital, and in this case he is fully right in saying: "A profit of 400 per cent will be sacrificed to a loss of 35 per cent." After establishing this strange proposition as a mathematician, he gives us the explanation of it as an economist.

"A social profit equal to 400 represents for the individual, in a society of only a million men, four ten-thousandths." Agreed; but we are dealing not with 400, but with 400 per cent, and a profit of 400 per cent represents for the individual 400 per cent, neither more nor less. Whatever be the capital, the dividends will always be in the ratio of 400 per cent. What does M. Proudhon do? He takes percentages for capital, and, as if he were afraid of his confusion not being manifest enough, "pointed" enough, he continues:

"A loss of 33 per cent for the consumer would suppose a social deficit of 33 millions." A loss of 33 per cent for the consumer remains a loss of 33 per cent for a million consumers. How then can M. Proudhon say pertinently that the social deficit in the case of a 33 per cent loss amounts to 33 millions, when he knows neither the social capital nor even the capital of a single one of the persons concerned? Thus it was not enough for M. Proudhon to have confused *capital with percentage;* he surpasses himself by identifying the *capital* sunk in an enterprise with the *number* of interested parties.

"To bring the matter home still more pointedly let us suppose in fact" a given capital. A social profit of 400 per cent divided among a million participants, each of them interested to the extent of one franc, would give 4 francs profit per head—and not 0.0004, as M. Proudhon alleges. Likewise a loss of 33 per cent for each of the participants represents a social deficit of 330,000 francs and not of 33 millions (100:33=1,000,000:330,000).

M. Proudhon, preoccupied with his theory of the person-society, forgets to divide by 100, which entails a loss of 330,000 francs; but 4 francs profit per head makes 4 million francs profit for society. There remains for society a net profit of 3,670,000 francs. This accurate calculation proves precisely the contrary of that which M. Proudhon wanted to prove: namely, that the profits and losses of society are not in inverse ratio to the profits and losses of individuals.

Having rectified these simple errors of pure calculation, let us take a look at the consequences which we would arrive at, if we admitted this relation between speed and capital in the case of railways, as M. Proudhon gives it—minus the mistakes in calculation. Let us suppose that a transport four times as rapid costs four times as much; this transport would not yield less profit than cartage, which is four times slower and costs a quarter the amount. Thus, if cartage takes 18 centimes, rail transport could take 72 centimes. This would be, according to "the rigour of mathematics," the consequence of M. Proudhon's suppositions— always minus his mistakes in calculation. But here he is all of a sudden telling us that if, instead of 72 centimes, rail transport takes only 25, it would instantly lose all its consignments. Decidedly we should have to go back to the van, to the primitive waggon even. Only, if we have any advice to give M. Proudhon, it is not to forget, in his *Programme of the Progressive Association,* to divide by 100. But, alas! it is scarcely to be hoped that our advice will be listened to, for M. Proudhon is so delighted with his "progressive" calculation, corresponding to the "progressive association," that he cries most emphatically:

> I have already shown in Chapter II, by the solution of the antinomy of value, that the advantage of every useful discovery is incomparably less for the inventor, whatever he may do, than for society. I have carried the demonstration in regard to this point *to the rigour of* mathematics!

Let us return to the fiction of the person-society, a fiction which has no other aim than that of proving this simple truth— that a new invention which enables a given amount of labour to produce a greater number of commodities, lowers the marketable value of the product. Society, then, makes a profit, not by obtaining more exchange values, but by obtaining more commodities for the same value. As for the inventor, competition makes his profit fall successively to the general level of profits. Has M. Proudhon proved this proposition as he wanted to? No. This does not prevent him from reproaching the economists with failure to prove it. To prove to him on the contrary that they *have* proved it, we shall cite only Ricardo and Lauderdale—Ricardo, the head of the school which determines value by labour time, and Lauderdale, one of the most uncompromising defenders of the determination of value by supply and demand. Both have expounded the same proposition:

> By constantly increasing the facility of production, we constantly diminish the value of some of the commodities before produced, though by the same means we not only add to the national riches, but also to the power of future production.... As soon as by the aid of machinery, or by the knowledge of natural philosophy, you oblige natural agents to do the work which was before done by man, the exchangeable value of such work falls accord-

ingly. If ten men turned a corn mill, and it be discovered that by the assistance of wind, or of water, the labour of these ten men may be spared, the flour which is the produce partly of the work performed by the mill, would immediately fall in value, in proportion to the quantity of labour saved; and the society would be richer by the commodities which the labour of the ten men could produce, the funds destined for their maintenance being in no degree impaired. (Ricardo [II:59].)

Lauderdale, in his turn, says:

In every instance where capital is so employed as to produce a profit, it uniformly arises, either—from its supplanting a portion of labour, which would otherwise be performed by the hand of man; or—from its performing a portion of labour, which is beyond the reach of the personal exertion of man to accomplish. The small profit which the proprietors of machinery generally acquire, when compared with the wages of labour, which the machine supplants, may perhaps create a suspicion of the rectitude of this opinion. Some fire-engines, for instance, draw more water from a coal-pit in one day, than could be conveyed on the shoulders of three hundred men, even assisted by the machinery of buckets; and a fire-engine undoubtedly performs its labour at a much smaller expense than the amount of the wages of those whose labour it thus supplants. This is, in truth, the case with all machinery. All machines must execute the labour that was antecedently performed at a cheaper rate than it could be done by the hand of man.... If such a privilege is given for the invention of a machine, which performs, by the labour of one man, a quantity of work that used to take the labour of four; as the possession of the exclusive privilege prevents any competition in doing the work, but what proceeds from the labour of the workmen, their wages, as long as the patent continues, must obviously form the measure of the patentee's charge; that is to secure employment, he has only to charge a little less than the wages of the labour which the machine supplants. But when the patent expires, other machines of the same nature are brought into competition; and then his charge must be regulated on the same principle as every other, according to the abundance of machines.... The profit of capital employed.... though it arises from supplanting labour, comes to be regulated, not by the value of the labour it supplants, but, as in all other cases, by the competition among the proprietors of capital; and it will be great or small in proportion to the quantity of capital that presents itself for performing the duty, and the demand for it. [Pp. 119, 123, 124, 125, 134.]

Finally, then, so long as the profit is greater than in other industries, capital will be thrown into the new industry until the rate of profit falls to the general level.

We have just seen that the example of the railway was scarcely suited to throw any light on his fiction of the person-society. Nevertheless, M. Proudhon boldly resumes his discourse: "With these points cleared up, nothing is easier than to explain how labour must leave a surplus for each producer." [I: 77]

What now follows belongs to classical antiquity. It is a poetical narrative intended to refresh the reader after the fatigue which the rigour of the preceding mathematical demonstrations must have caused him. M. Proudhon gives the person-society, the name of *Prometheus,* whose high deeds he glorifies in these terms:

> First of all, Prometheus emerging from the bosom of nature awakes to life, in a delightful inertia, etc., etc. Prometheus sets to work, and on this first day, the first day of the second creation, Prometheus' product, that is, his wealth, his well-being, is equal to ten. On the second day, Prometheus divides his labour, and his product becomes equal to a hundred. On the third day and on each of the following days, Prometheus invents machines, discovers new utilities in bodies, new forces in nature.... With every step of his industrial activity, there is an increase in the number of his products, which marks an enhancement of happiness for him. And since, after all, to consume is for him to produce, it is clear that every day's consumption. using up only the product of the day before, leaves a surplus product for the next day. [I: 77-78]

This Prometheus of M. Proudhon's is a queer character, as weak in logic as in political economy. So long as Prometheus merely teaches us the division of labour, the application of machinery, the exploitation of natural forces and scientific power, multiplying the productive forces of men and giving a surplus compared with the produce of labour in isolation, this new Prometheus has the misfortune only of coming too late. But the moment Prometheus starts talking about production and consumption he becomes really ludicrous.

To consume, for him, is to produce; he consumes the next day what he produced the day before, so that he is always one day in advance; this day in advance is his "surplus labour." But, if he consumes the next day what he has produced the day before, he must, on the first day, which had no day before, have done two days' work in order to be one day in advance later on. How did Prometheus earn this surplus on the first day, when there was neither division of labour, nor machinery, nor even any knowledge of physical forces other than fire? Thus the question, for all its being carried back "to the first day of the second creation," has not advanced a single step forward. This way of explaining things savours both of Greek and of Hebrew, it is at once mystical and allegorical. It gives M. Proudhon a perfect right to say: "I have proved by theory and by facts the principle that all labour must have a surplus." The "facts" are the famous progressive Calculation; the theory is the myth of Prometheus. Continues M. Proudhon:

> "But this principle, while being as certain as an arithmetical proposition, is as yet far from being realized by everyone. Whereas, with the progress of collective industry, every day's individual labour produces a greater and greater product, and whereas therefore, by a necessary consequence, the

worker with the same wage ought to become richer every day, there actually exist estates in society which profit and others which decay. [I: 79-80]

In 1770 the population of the United Kingdom of Great Britain was 15 million, and the productive population was 3 million. The scientific power of production equalled a population of about 12 million individuals more. Therefore there were, altogether, 15 million of productive forces. Thus the productive power was to the population as 1 is to 1; and the scientific power was to the manual power as 4 is to 1.

In 1840 the population did not exceed 30 million: the productive population was 6 million. But the scientific power amounted to 650 million; that is, it was to the whole population as 21 is to 1, and to manual power as 108 is to 1.

In English society the working day thus acquired in seventy years a surplus of 2,700 per cent productivity; that is, in 1840 it produced 27 times as much as in 1770. According to M. Proudhon, the following question should be raised: why was not the English worker of 1840 twenty-seven times as rich as the one of 1770? In raising such a question one would naturally be supposing that the English could have produced this wealth without the historical conditions in which it was produced, such as: private accumulation of capital, modern division of labour, automatic workshops, anarchical competition, the wage system—in short, everything that is based upon class antagonism. Now, these were precisely the necessary conditions of existence for the development of productive forces and of surplus labour.

Therefore, to obtain this development of productive forces and this surplus labour, there had to be classes which profited and classes which decayed.

What then, ultimately, is this Prometheus resuscitated by M. Proudhon? It is society, social relations based on class antagonism. These relations are not relations between individual and individual, but between worker and capitalist, between farmer and landlord, etc. Wipe out these relations and you annihilate all society, and your Prometheus is nothing but a ghost without arms or legs; that is, without automatic workshops, without division of labour—in a word, without everything that you gave him to start with in order to make him obtain this surplus labour.

If then, in theory, it sufficed to interpret, as M. Proudhon does, the formula of surplus labour in the equalitarian sense, without taking into account the actual conditions of production, it should suffice, in practice, to share out equally among the workers all the wealth at present acquired, without changing in any way the present conditions of production. Such a distribution would certainly not assure a high degree of comfort to the individual participants.

But M. Proudhon is not so pessimistic as one might think. As proportion is everything for him, he has to see in his fully equipped Prometheus, that is, in present-day society, the beginnings of a realization of his favourite idea.

> But everywhere, too, the progress of wealth, that is, *the proportion of values,* is the dominant law; and when economists hold up against the complaints of the social party the progressive growth of the public wealth, and the improved conditions of even the most unfortunate classes, they unwittingly proclaim a truth which is the condemnation of their theories. [I: 80]

What is, actually, collective wealth, public fortune? It is the wealth of the bourgeoisie- not that of each bourgeois in particular. Well, the economists have done nothing but show how, in the existing relations of production, the wealth of the bourgeoisie has grown and must grow still further. As for the working classes, it still remains a very debatable question whether their condition has improved as a result of the increase in so-called public wealth. If economists, in support of their optimism. cite the example of the English workers employed in the cotton industry, they see the condition of the latter only in the rare moments of trade prosperity. These moments of prosperity are to the periods of crisis and stagnation in the "true proportion" of 3 to 10. But perhaps also, in speaking of improvement, the economists were thinking of the millions of workers who had to perish in the East Indies so as to procure for the million and a half workers employed in England in the same industry, three years' prosperity out of ten.

As for the temporary participation in the increase of public wealth, that is a different matter. The fact of temporary participation is explained by the theory of the economists. It is the confirmation of this theory and not its "condemnation," as M. Proudhon calls it. If there were anything to be condemned, it would surely be the system of M. Proudhon, who would reduce the worker, as we have shown, to the minimum wage, in spite of the increase in wealth. It is only by reducing the worker to the minimum wage that he would be able to apply the true proportion of values, of "value constituted"—by labour time. It is because wages, as a result of competition, oscillate now above, now below, the price of food necessary for the sustenance of the worker, that he can participate to a certain extent in the development of collective wealth, and can also perish from want. This is the whole theory of the economists who have no illusions on the subject.

After his lengthy digressions on railways, on Prometheus, and on the new society to be reconstituted on "constituted value," M. Proudhon collects himself; emotion overpowers him and he cries in fatherly tones:

> I *beseech* the economists to ask themselves for one moment, in the silence of their hearts—far from the prejudices that trouble them and regardless of the employment they are engaged in or hope to obtain, of the interests they subserve, or the approbation to which they aspire, of the honours which nurse their vanity—let them say whether before this day the principle that all labour must leave a surplus appeared to them with this chain of premises and consequences that we have revealed. [I: 80]

CHAPTER II

THE METAPHYSICS OF POLITICAL ECONOMY

§1. THE METHOD

Here we are, right in Germany! We shall now have to talk metaphysics while talking political economy. And in this again we shall but follow M. Proudhon's "contradictions." Just now he forced us to speak English, to become pretty well English ourselves. Now the scene is changing. M. Proudhon is transporting us to our dear fatherland and is forcing us, whether we like it or not, become German again.

If the Englishman transforms men into hats, the German transforms hats into ideas. The Englishman is Ricardo, rich banker and distinguished economist; the German is Hegel, simple professor of philosophy at the University of Berlin.

Louis XV, the last absolute monarch and representative of the decadence of French royalty, had attached to his person a physician who was himself France's first economist. This doctor, this economist, represented the imminent and certain triumph of the French bourgeoisie. Doctor Quesnay made a science out of political economy; he summarized it in his famous *Tableau économique*. Besides the thousand and one commentaries on this table which have appeared, we possess one by the doctor himself. It is the "analysis of the economic table," followed by "seven *important observations*."[22]

M. Proudhon is another Dr. Quesnay. He is the Quesnay of the metaphysics of political economy.

Now metaphysics—indeed all philosophy—can be summed up, according to Hegel, in method. We must, therefore, try to elucidate the method of M. Proudhon, which is at least as foggy as the *Economic Table*. It is for this reason that we are making seven more or less important observations. If Dr. Proudhon is not pleased with our observations, well, then, he will have to become an Abbe Baudeau and give the "explanation of the economico-metaphysical method" himself.[23]

76

First Observation

We are not giving a *history according to the order in time, but according to the sequence of ideas.* Economic *phases or categories* are in their *manifestation* sometimes contemporary, sometimes inverted.... Economic theories have none the less their *logical sequence* and their *serial relation in the understanding:* it is this order that we flatter ourselves to have discovered. (Proudhon, Vol. I, p. 146.)

M. Proudhon most certainly wanted to frighten the French by flinging quasi-Hegelian phrases at them. So we have to deal with two men: firstly with M. Proudhon, and then with Hegel. How does M. Proudhon distinguish himself from other economists? And what part does Hegel play in M. Proudhon's political economy?

Economists express the relations of bourgeois production, the division of labour, credit, money, etc., as fixed, immutable, eternal categories. M. Proudhon, who has these ready-made categories before him, wants to explain to us the act of formation, the genesis of these categories, principles, laws, ideas, thoughts.

Economists explain how production takes place in the abovementioned relations, but what they do not explain is how these relations themselves are produced, that is, the historical movement which gave, them birth.

M. Proudhon, taking these relations for principles, categories, abstract thoughts, has merely to put into *order* these thoughts, which are to be found alphabetically arranged at the end of every treatise on political economy. The economists' material is the active, energetic life of man; M. Proudhon's material is the dogmas of the economists. But the moment we cease to pursue the historical movement of production relations, of which the categories are but the theoretical expression, the moment we want to see in these categories no more than ideas, spontaneous thoughts, independent of real relations, we are forced to attribute the origin of these thoughts to the movement of pure reason. How does pure, eternal, impersonal reason give rise to these thoughts? How does it proceed in order to produce them?

If we had M. Proudhon's intrepidity in the matter of Hegelianism we should say: it is distinguished in itself from itself. What does this mean? Impersonal reason, having -outside itself neither a base on which it can pose itself, nor an object to which it can oppose itself, nor a subject with which it can compose itself, is forced to turn head over heels, in posing itself, opposing itself and composing itself—position, opposition, composition. Or, to speak Greek—we have thesis, antithesis and synthesis. For those who do not know the Hegelian language, we shall give the

consecrating formula:—affirmation, negation and negation of the
negation. That is what language means. It is certainly not Hebrew (with due apologies to M. Proudhon); but it is the language
of this pure reason, separate from the individual. Instead of the
ordinary individual with his ordinary manner of speaking and
thinking we have nothing but this ordinary manner in itself—
without the individual.

Is it surprising that everything, in the final abstraction—for
we have here an abstraction, and not an analysis—presents itself
as a logical category? Is it surprising that, if you let drop little by
little all that constitutes the individuality of a house., leaving out
first of all the materials of which it is composed, then the form
that distinguishes it, you end up with nothing but a body; that, if
you leave out of account the limits of this body, you soon have
nothing but a space—that if, finally, you leave out of account the
dimensions of this space, there is absolutely nothing left but pure
quantity, the logical category? If we abstract thus from every
subject all the alleged accidents, animate or inanimate, men or
things, we are right in saying that in the final abstraction, the
only substance left is the logical categories. Thus the metaphysicians who, in making these abstractions, think they are making
analyses, and who, the more they detach themselves from things,
imagine themselves to be getting all the nearer to the point of
penetrating to their core—these metaphysicians in turn are right
in saying that things here below are embroideries of which the,
logical categories constitute the canvas. This is what distinguishes the philosopher from the Christian. The Christian, in
spite of logic, has only one incarnation of the *Logos;* the philosopher has never finished with incarnations. If all that exists, all
that lives on land and under water can be reduced by abstraction
to a logical category—if the whole real world can be drowned
thus in a world of abstractions, in the world of logical categories—who need be astonished at it?

All that exists, all that lives on land and under water, exists
and lives only by some kind of movement. Thus the movement of
history produces social relations; industrial movement gives us
industrial products, etc.

Just as by dint of abstraction we have transformed everything
into a logical category, so one has only to make an abstraction of
every characteristic distinctive of different movements to attain
movement in its abstract condition—purely formal movement,
the purely logical formula of movement. If one finds in logical
categories the substance of all things, one imagines one has
found in the logical formula of movement the *absolute method,*

which not only explains all things, but also implies the movement of things.

It is of this absolute method that Hegel speaks in these terms:

> Method is the absolute, unique, supreme, infinite force, which no object can resist; it is the tendency of reason to find itself again, to recognize itself in every object. (*Logic*, Vol. III.[24])

All things being reduced to a logical category, and every movement, every act of production, to method, it follows naturally that every aggregate of products and production, of objects and of movement, can be reduced to. a form of applied metaphysics. What Hegel has done for religion, law, etc., M. Proudhon seeks to do for political economy.

So what is this absolute method? The abstraction of movement. What is the abstraction of movement? Movement in abstract condition. What is movement in abstract condition? The purely logical formula of movement or the movement of pure reason. Wherein does the movement of pure reason consist? In posing itself, opposing itself, composing itself; in formulating itself as thesis, antithesis, synthesis; or, yet again, in affirming itself, negating itself and negating its negation.

How does reason manage to affirm itself, to pose it. self in a definite category? That is the business of reason itself and of its apologists.

But once it has managed to pose itself as a thesis, this thesis, this thought, opposed to itself, splits up into two contradictory thoughts—the positive and the negative, the yes and the no. The struggle between these two antagonistic elements comprised in the antithesis constitutes the dialectical movement. The yes becoming no, the no becoming yes, the yes becoming both yes and no, the no becoming both no and yes, the contraries balance, neutralize, paralyse each other. The fusion of these two contradictory thoughts constitutes a new thought, which is the synthesis of them. This thought splits up once again into two contradictory thoughts, which in turn fuse into a new synthesis. Of this travail is born a group of thoughts. This group of thoughts follows the same dialectic movement as the simple category, and has a contradictory group as antithesis. Of these two groups of thoughts is born a new group of thoughts, which is the synthesis of them.

Just as from the dialectic movement of the simple categories is born the group, so from the dialectic movement of the groups is born the series, and from the dialectic movement of the series is born the entire system.

Apply this method to the categories of political economy, and you have the logic and metaphysics of political economy, or, in other words, you have the economic categories that everybody knows, translated into a little-known language which makes them look as if they had newly blossomed forth in an intellect of pure reason; so much do these categories seem to engender one another, to be linked up and intertwined with one another by the very working of the dialectic movement The reader must not get alarmed at these metaphysics with all their scaffolding of categories, groups, series and systems. M. Proudhon, in spite of all the trouble he has taken to scale the heights of the *system of contradictions,* has never been able to raise himself above the first two rungs of simple thesis and antithesis; and even these he has mounted only twice, and on one of these two occasions he fell over backwards.

Up to now we have expounded only the dialectics of Hegel. We shall see later how M. Proudhon has succeeded in reducing it to the meanest proportions. Thus, for Hegel, all that has happened and is still happening is only just what is happening in his own mind. Thus the philosophy of history is nothing but the history of philosophy, of his own philosophy. There is no longer a "history according to the order in time," there is only "the sequence of ideas in the understanding." He thinks he is constructing the world by the movement of thought, whereas he is merely reconstructing systematically and classifying by the absolute method the thoughts which are in the minds of all.

Second Observation

Economic categories are only the theoretical expressions, the abstractions of the social relations of production. M. Proudhon, holding things upside down like a true philosopher, sees in actual relations nothing but the incarnation of these principles, of these categories, which were slumbering—so M. Proudhon the philosopher tells us—in the bosom of the "impersonal reason of humanity."

M. Proudhon the economist understands very well that men make cloth, linen or silk materials in definite relations of production. But what he has not understood is that these definite social relations are just as much produced by men as linen, flax, etc. Social relations are closely bound up with productive forces. In acquiring new productive forces men change their mode of production; and in changing their mode of production, in changing the way of earning their living, they change all their social relations. The handmill gives you society with the feudal lord; the steam-mill, society with the industrial capitalist.

The same men who establish their social relations in conformity with their material productivity, produce also principles, ideas and categories, in conformity with their social relations.

Thus these ideas, these categories, are as little eternal as the relations they express. They are *historical and transitory products*.

There is a continual movement of growth in productive forces, of destruction in social relations, of formation in ideas; the only immutable thing is the abstraction of movement—*mors immortalis*.[25]

Third Observation

The production relations of every society form a whole. M. Proudhon considers economic relations as so many social phases, engendering one another, resulting one from the other like the antithesis from the thesis, and realizing in their logical sequence the impersonal reason of humanity.

The only drawback to this method is that when he comes to examine a single one of these phases, M. Proudhon cannot explain it without having recourse to all the other relations of society; which relations, however, he has not yet made his dialectic movement engender. When, after that, M. Proudhon, by means of pure reason, proceeds to give birth to these other phases, he treats them as if they were new-born babes. He forgets that they are of the same age as the first.

Thus, to arrive at the constitution of value, which for him is the basis of all economic evolutions, he could not do without division of labour, competition, etc. Yet in the *series*, in the *understanding* of M. Proudhon, in the *logical sequence*, these relations did not yet exist.

In constructing the edifice of an ideological system by means of the categories of political economy, the limbs of the social system are dislocated. The different limbs of society are converted into so many separate societies, following one upon the other. How, indeed, could the single logical formula of movement, of sequence, of time, explain the structure of society, in which all relations coexist simultaneously and support one another?

Fourth Observation

Let us see now to what modifications M. Proudhon subjects Hegel's dialectics when he applies it to political economy.

For him, M. Proudhon, every economic category has two sides—one good, the other bad. He looks upon these categories as the petty bourgeois looks upon the great men of history: *Napoleon* was a great man; he did a lot of good; he also did a lot of harm.

The *good side* and the *bad side, the advantages and the drawbacks,* taken together form for M. Proudhon the *contradiction* in every economic category.

The problem to be solved: to keep the good side, while eliminating the bad.

Slavery is an economic category like any other. Thus it also has its two sides. Let us leave alone the bad side and talk about the good side of slavery. Needless to say we are dealing only with direct slavery, with Negro slavery in Surinam, in Brazil, in the Southern States of North America.

Direct slavery is just as much the pivot of bourgeois industry as machinery, credits, etc. Without slavery you have no cotton; without cotton you have no modern industry. It is slavery that gave the colonies their value; it is the colonies that created world trade, and it is world trade that is the precondition of large-scale industry. Thus slavery is an economic category of the greatest importance.

Without slavery North America, the most progressive of countries, would be transformed into a patriarchal country. Wipe North America off the map of the world, and you will have anarchy—the complete decay of modern commerce and civilization. Cause slavery to disappear and you will have wiped America off the map of nations.*

Thus slavery, because it is an economic category, has always existed among the institutions of the peoples. Modern nations have been able only to disguise slavery in their own countries, but they have imposed it without disguise upon the New World.

What would M. Proudhon do to save slavery? He would formulate the *problem* thus: preserve the good side of this economic category, eliminate the bad.

Hegel has no problems to formulate. He has only dialectics. M. Proudhon has nothing of Hegel's dialectics but the language. For

---

* This was perfectly correct for the year 1847. At that time the world trade of the United States was limited mainly to import of immigrants and industrial products, and export of cotton and tobacco, i.e., of the products of southern slave labour. The Northern States produced mainly corn and meat for the slave states. It was only when the North produced corn and meat for export and also became an industrial country, and when the American cotton monopoly had to face powerful competition, in India, Egypt, Brazil, etc., that the abolition of slavery became possible. And even then this led to the ruin of the South, which did not succeed in replacing the open Negro slavery by the disguised slavery of Indian and Chinese coolies *(Note by F. Engels to the German edition, 1885.]*

him the dialectic movement is the dogmatic distinction between good and bad.

Let us for a moment consider M. Proudhon himself as a category. Let us examine his good and his bad side, his advantages and his drawbacks.

If he has the advantage over Hegel of setting problems which he reserves the right of solving for the greater good of humanity, he has the drawback of being stricken with sterility when it is a question of engendering a new category by dialectical birth-throes. What constitutes dialectical movement is the coexistence of two contradictory sides, their conflict and their fusion into a new category. The very setting of the problem of eliminating the bad side cuts short the dialectic movement. It is not the category which is posed and opposed to itself, by its contradictory nature, it is M. Proudhon who gets excited, perplexed and frets and fumes between the two sides of the category.

Caught thus in a blind alley, from which it is difficult to escape by legal means, M. Proudhon takes a real flying leap which transports him at one bound into a new category. Then it is that to his astonished gaze is revealed the *serial relation in the understanding.*

He takes the first category that comes handy and attributes to it arbitrarily the quality of supplying a remedy for the drawbacks of the category to be purified. Thus, if we are to believe M. Proudhon, taxes remedy the drawbacks of monopoly; the balance of trade, the drawbacks of taxes; landed property, the drawbacks of credit.

By taking the economic categories thus successively, one by one, and making one the *antidote* to the other, M. Proudhon manages to make with this mixture of contradictions and antidotes to contradictions, two volumes of contradictions, which he rightly entitles: *The System of Economic Contradictions.*

Fifth Observation

In the absolute reason all these ideas ... are equally simple, and general.... In fact, we attain knowledge only by a *sort of scaffolding* of our ideas. But truth in itself is independent of these dialectical symbols and freed from the combinations of our minds. (Proudhon, Vol. II, p. 97.)

Here all of a sudden, by a kind of switch-over of which we now know the secret, the metaphysics of political economy has become an illusion! Never has M. Proudhon spoken more truly. Indeed, from the moment the process of the dialectic movement is reduced to the simple process of opposing good to bad, of posing problems tending to eliminate the bad, and of administering one category as an antidote to another, the categories are deprived of all spontaneity; the idea "ceases *to* function"; there is no life left in it. It is no longer posed or decomposed into categories. The sequence of categories has become a *sort of scaffolding*. Dialectics has ceased to be the movement of absolute reason. There is no longer any dialectics but only, at the most, absolutely pure morality.

When M. Proudhon spoke of the *series in the understanding*, of the *logical sequence of categories*, he declared positively that he did not want to give *history according to the order in time*, that is, in M. Proudhon's view, the historical sequence in which the categories *have manifested* themselves. Thus for him everything happened in the *pure ether of reason*. Everything was to be derived from this ether by means of dialectics. Now that he has to put this dialectics into practice, his reason is in default. M. Proudhon's dialectics runs counter to Hegel's dialectics, and now we have M. Proudhon reduced to saying that the order in which he gives the economic categories is no longer the order in which they engender one another. Economic evolutions are no longer the evolutions of reason itself.

What then does M. Proudhon give us? Peal history, which is, according to M. Proudhon's understanding, the sequence in which the categories have *manifested* themselves in order of time? No! History as it takes place in the idea itself? Still less! That is, neither the profane history of the categories, nor their sacred history! What history does he give us then? The history of his own contradictions. Let us see how they go, and how they drag M. Proudhon in their train.

Before entering upon this examination, which gives rise to the sixth important observation, we have yet another, less important observation to make.

Let us admit with M. Proudhon that real history, history according to the order in time, is the historical sequence in which ideas, categories and principles have manifested themselves.

Each principle has had its own century in which to manifest itself. The principle of authority, for example, had the eleventh century, just as the principle of individualism had the eighteenth century. In logical sequence, it was the century that belonged to the principle, and not the principle that belonged to the century. In other words it was the principle that made the history, and not the history that made the principle. When, consequently, in order to save principles as much as to save history, we ask ourselves why a particular principle was manifested in the eleventh or in the eighteenth century rather than in any other, we are necessarily forced to examine minutely what men were like in the eleventh century, what they were like in the eighteenth, what were their respective needs, their productive forces, their mode of production, the raw materials of their production—in short, what were the relations between man and man which resulted from all these conditions of existence. To get to the bottom of all these questions—what is this but to draw up the real, profane history of men in every century and to present these men as both the authors and the actors of their own drama? But the moment you present men as the actors and authors of their own history, you arrive—by a detour—at the real starting point, because you have abandoned those eternal principles of which you spoke at the outset.

M. Proudhon has not even gone far enough along the, crossroad which an ideologist takes to reach the main road of history.

Sixth Observation

Let us take the sideroad with M. Proudhon.

We shall concede that economic relations, viewed as *immutable laws, eternal principles, ideal categories,* existed before active and energetic men did; we shall concede further that these laws, principles and categories had, since the beginning of time, slumbered "in the impersonal reason of humanity." We have already seen that, with all these changeless and motionless eternities, there is no history left; there is at most history in the idea, that is, history reflected in the dialectic movement of pure reason. M. Proudhon, by saying that, in the dialectic movement, ideas are no longer *differentiated,* has done away with both the *shadow of movement* and the *movement of shadows,* by means of which one could still have created at least a semblance of history. Instead of that, he imputes to history his own impotence. He lays the blame on everything, even the French language. "It is inexact then," says M. Proudhon, the philosopher, "to say that something *appears,* that something *is produced:* in civilization as in the universe, everything has existed, has acted, from eternity. *This applies to the whole of social economy."* (Vol. II, p. 102.)

So great is the productive force of the contradictions which *function* and which make M. Proudhon function, that, in trying to explain history, he is forced to deny it; in trying to explain the successive appearance of social relations, he denies that *anything can appear: in* trying to explain production, with all its phases, he questions whether *anything can be produced!*

Thus, for M. Proudhon, there is no longer any history: no longer any sequence of ideas. And yet his book still exists; and it is precisely that book which is, to use his own expression, *"history according to the sequence of ideas."* How shall we find a formula, for M. Proudhon is a man of formulas, to help him to clear all these contradictions *in one leap?*

To this end he has invented a new reason, which is neither the pure and virgin absolute reason, nor the common reason of men living and acting in different periods, but a reason quite apart— the reason of the person, Society-of the subject, Humanity— which under the pen of M. Proudhon figures at times also as *social genius, general reason,* or finally as *human reason.* This reason, decked out under so many names, betrays itself never- theless, at every moment, as the individual reason of M. Proud- hon, with its good and its bad side, its antidotes and its prob- lems.

"Human reason does not create truth," hidden in the depths of absolute, eternal reason. It can only unveil it. But such truths as it has unveiled up to now are incomplete, insufficient and conse- quently contradictory. Hence, economic categories, being them- selves truths discovered, revealed by human reason, by social genius, are equally incomplete and contain within themselves the germ of contradiction. Before M. Proudhon, social genius saw only the *antagonistic elements,* and not the *synthetic formula,* both hidden simultaneously in *absolute reason.* Economic rela- tions, which merely realize on earth these insufficient truths, these incomplete categories, these contradictory ideas, are conse- quently contradictory in themselves, and present two sides, one good, the other bad.

To find complete truth, the idea, in all its fullness, the syn- thetic formula that is to annihilate the contradiction, this is the problem of social genius. This again is why, in M. Proudhon's illusion, this same social genius has been harried from one cate- gory to another without ever having been able, despite all its battery of categories, to snatch from God or from absolute rea- son, a synthetic formula.

At first, society (social genius) states a primary fact, puts forward a *hypothesis...* a veritable antinomy, whose antagonistic results develop in the social economy in the same way as its consequences could have been deduced in the mind; so that industrial movement, following in all things the deduction of ideas, splits up into two currents, one of useful effects, the other of subversive results. To bring harmony into the constitution of this two-sided principle, and to solve this antinomy, society gives rise to a *second,* which will soon be followed by a third; and *progress of social genius will* take place in this manner, until, having exhausted all its contradic- tions—I suppose, but it is not proved that there is a limit to human contradictions—it returns in one leap to all its former positions and *with a single formula* solves all its problems. (Vol. I, p. 133.)

Just as the *antithesis* was before turned into an *antidote*, so now the *thesis* becomes a *hypothesis*. *This* change of terms, coming from M. Proudhon, has no longer anything surprising for us! Human reason, which is anything but pure, having only incomplete vision, encounters at every step new problems to be solved. Every new thesis which it discovers in absolute reason and which is the negation of the first thesis, becomes for it a synthesis, which it accepts rather naively as the solution of the problem in question. It is thus that this reason frets and fumes in ever renewing contradictions until, coming to the end of the contradictions, it perceives that all its theses and syntheses are merely contradictory hypotheses. In its perplexity, "human reason, social genius, returns in one leap to all its former positions, and in a single formula, solves all its problems." This unique formula, by the way, constitutes M. Proudhon's true discovery. It is constituted value.

Hypotheses are made only in view of a certain aim. The aim that social genius, speaking through the mouth of M. Proudhon, set itself in the first place, was to eliminate the bad in every economic category, in order to have nothing left but the good. For it, the good, the supreme well-being, the real practical aim, is *equality*. And why did the social genius aim at equality rather than inequality, fraternity, Catholicism, or any other principle? Because "humanity his successively realized so many separate hypotheses only in view of a superior hypothesis," which precisely is equality. In other words: because equality is M. Proudhon's ideal. He imagines that the division of labour, credit, the workshop,—all economic relations—were invented merely for the benefit of equality, and yet they always ended up by turning against it. Since history and the fiction of M. Proudhon contradict each other at every step, the latter concludes that there is a contradiction. If there is a contradiction, it exists only between his fixed idea and real movement.

Henceforth the good side of an economic relation is that which affirms equality; the bad side, that which negates it and affirms inequality. Every new category is a hypothesis of the social genius to eliminate the inequality engendered by the preceding hypothesis. In short, equality is the *primordial intention, the mystical tendency, the providential aim* that the social genius has constantly before its eyes as it whirls in the circle of economic contradictions. Thus *Providence* is the locomotive which makes the whole of M. Proudhon's economic baggage move better than his pure and volatilized reason. He has devoted to Providence a whole chapter, which follows the one on taxes.[26]

Providence, providential aim, this is the great word used to-day to explain the movement of history. In fact, this word explains nothing. It is at most a rhetorical form, one of the various ways of paraphrasing facts.

It is a fact that in Scotland landed property acquired a new value by the development of English industry. This industry opened up new outlets for wool. In order to produce wool on a large scale, arable land had to be transformed into pasturage. To effect this transformation, the estates had to be concentrated. To concentrate the estates, small holdings had first to be abolished, thousands of tenants had to be driven from their native soil and a few shepherds in charge of millions of sheep to be installed in their place. Thus, by successive transformations, landed property in Scotland has resulted in the driving out of men by sheep. Now say that the providential aim of the institution of landed property in Scotland was to have men driven out by sheep, and you will have made providential history.

Of course, the tendency towards equality belongs to our century. To say now that all former centuries, with entirely different needs, means of production, etc., worked providentially for the realization of equality is, firstly, to substitute the means and the men of our century for the men and the means of earlier centuries and to misunderstand the historical movement by which the successive generations transformed the results acquired by the generations that preceded them. Economists know very well that the very thing that was for the one a finished product was for the other but the raw material for new production.

Suppose, as M. Proudhon does, that social genius produced, or rather improvised, the feudal lords with the providential aim of transforming the *settlers into responsible and equally-placed* workers: and you will have effected a substitution of aims and of persons worthy of the Providence that instituted landed property in Scotland, in order to give itself the malicious pleasure of driving out men by sheep.

But since M. Proudhon takes such a tender interest in Providence, we refer him to the *Histoire de l'Economie politique* of M. de Villeneuve-Bargemont,[27] who likewise goes in pursuit of a providential aim. This aim, however, is not equality, but Catholicism.

Seventh and Last Observation

Economists have a singular method of procedure.

There are only two kinds of institutions for them, artificial and natural. The institutions of feudalism are artificial institutions, those of the bourgeoisie are natural institutions. In this they resemble the theologians, who likewise establish two kinds of religion. Every religion which is not theirs is an invention of men, while their own is an emanation from God. When the economists say that present-day relations—the relations of bourgeois production—are natural, they imply that these are the relations in which wealth is created and productive forces developed in conformity with the laws of nature. These relations therefore are themselves natural laws independent of the influence of time. They are eternal laws which must always govern society. Thus there has been history, but there is no longer any. There has been history, since there were the institutions of feudalism, and in these institutions of feudalism we find quite different relations of production from those of bourgeois society, which the economists try to pass off as natural and as such, eternal.

Feudalism also had its proletariat—serfdom, which contained all the germs of the bourgeoisie. Feudal production also had two antagonistic elements which are likewise designated by the name of the *good side and* the *bad side* of feudalism, irrespective of the fact that it is always the bad side that in the end triumphs over the good side. It is the bad side that produces the movement which makes history, by providing a struggle. If, during the epoch of the domination of feudalism, the economists, enthusiastic over the knightly virtues, the beautiful harmony between rights and duties, the patriarchal life of the towns, the prosperous condition of domestic industry in the countryside, the development of industry organized into corporations, guilds and fraternities, in short, everything that constitutes the good side of feudalism, had set themselves the problem of eliminating everything that cast a shadow on this picture—serfdom, privileges, anarchy— what would have happened? All the elements which called forth the struggle would have been destroyed, and the development of the bourgeoisie nipped in the bud. One would have set oneself the absurd problem of eliminating history.

After the triumph of the bourgeoisie there was no longer any question of the good or the bad side of feudalism. The bourgeoisie took possession of the productive forces it had developed under feudalism. All the old economic forms, the corresponding civil relations, the political state which was the official expression of the old civil society, were smashed.

Thus feudal production, to be judged properly, must be considered as a mode of production founded on antagonism. It must be shown how wealth was produced within this antagonism, how the productive forces were developed at the same time as class antagonisms, how one of the classes, the bad side, the drawback of society, went on growing until the material conditions for its emancipation had attained full maturity. Is not this as good as saying that the mode of production, the relations in which productive forces are developed, are anything but eternal laws, but that they correspond to a definite development of men and of their productive forces, and that a change in men's productive forces necessarily brings about a change in their relations of production? As the main thing is not to be deprived of the fruits of civilization, of the acquired productive forces, the traditional forms in which they were produced must be smashed. From this moment the revolutionary class becomes conservative.

The bourgeoisie begins with a proletariat which is itself a relic of the proletariat[28] of feudal times. In the course of its historical development, the bourgeoisie necessarily develops its antagonistic character, which at first is more or less disguised, existing only in a latent state. As the bourgeoisie develops, there develops in its bosom a new proletariat, a modern proletariat, there develops a struggle between the proletarian class and the bourgeois class, a struggle which, before being felt, perceived, appreciated, understood, avowed and proclaimed aloud by both sides, expresses itself, to start with, merely in partial and momentary conflicts, in subversive acts. On the other hand, if all the members of the modern bourgeoisie have the same interests inasmuch as they form a class as against another class, they have opposite, antagonistic interests inasmuch as they stand face to face with one another. This opposition of interests results from the economic conditions of their bourgeois life. From day to day it thus becomes clearer that the production relations in which the bourgeoisie moves have not a simple, uniform character, but a dual character; that in the selfsame relations in which wealth is produced, poverty is produced also; that in the selfsame relations in which there is a development of the productive forces, there is also La force producing repression; that these relations produce *bourgeois wealth*, i.e., the wealth of the bourgeois class, only by continually annihilating the wealth of the individual members of this class and by producing an ever-growing proletariat.

The more the antagonistic character comes to light, the more the economists, the scientific representatives of bourgeois production, find themselves in conflict with their own theory; and different schools arise.

We have the *fatalist* economists, who in their theory are as indifferent to what they call the drawbacks of bourgeois production as the bourgeois themselves are in practice to the sufferings of the proletarians who help them to acquire wealth. In this fatalist school there ate Classics and Romantics. The Classics, like Adam Smith and Ricardo, represent a bourgeoisie which, while still struggling with the relics of feudal society, works only to purge economic relations of feudal taints, to increase the productive forces and to give a new upsurge to industry and commerce. The proletariat that takes part in this struggle and is absorbed in this feverish labour experiences only passing, accidental sufferings, and itself regards them as such. Economists like Adam Smith and Ricardo, who are the historians of this epoch, have no other mission than that of showing how wealth is acquired in bourgeois production relations, of formulating these relations into categories, into laws, and of showing how superior these laws, these categories, are for the production of wealth to the laws and categories of feudal society. Poverty is in their eyes merely the pang which accompanies every childbirth, in nature as in industry.

The Romantics belong to our own age, in which the bourgeoisie is in direct opposition to the proletariat; in which poverty is engendered in as great abundance as wealth. The economists now pose as blasé fatalists, who, from their elevated position, cast a proudly disdainful glance at the human machines who manufacture wealth. They copy all the developments given by their predecessors, and the indifference which in the latter was merely naivete becomes in them coquetry.

Next comes the *humanitarian school,* which sympathizes with the bad side of present-day production relations. It seeks, by way of easing its conscience, to palliate even if slightly the real contrasts; it sincerely deplores the distress of the proletariat, the unbridled competition of the bourgeois among themselves; it counsels the workers to be sober, to work hard and to have few children; it advises the bourgeois to put a reasoned ardour into production. The whole theory of this school rests on interminable distinctions between theory and practice, between principles and results, between idea and application, between form and content, between essence and reality, between right and fact, between the good side and the bad side.

The philanthropic school is the humanitarian school carried to perfection. It denies the necessity of antagonism; it wants to turn all men into bourgeois; it wants to realize theory in so far as it is distinguished from practice and contains no antagonism. It goes without saying that, in theory, it is easy to make an abstraction of the contradictions that are met with at every moment in ac-

tual reality. This theory would therefore become idealized reality. The philanthropists, then, want to retain the categories
which express bourgeois relations, without the antagonism
which constitutes them and is inseparable from them. They
think they are seriously fighting bourgeois practice, and they
are more bourgeois than the others.

Just as the *economists* are the scientific representatives of the
bourgeois class, so the *Socialists* and the *Communists* are the
theoreticians of the proletarian class. So long as the proletariat
is not yet sufficiently developed to constitute itself as a class, and
consequently so long as the struggle itself of the proletariat with
the bourgeoisie has not yet assumed a political character, and
the productive forces are not yet sufficiently developed in the
bosom of the bourgeoisie itself to enable us to catch a glimpse of
the material conditions necessary for the emancipation of the
proletariat and for the formation of a new society, these theoreticians are merely utopians who, to meet the wants of the oppressed classes, improvise systems and go in search of a regenerating science. But in the measure that history moves forward,
and with it the struggle of the proletariat assumes clearer out-
lines, they no longer need to seek science in their minds; they
have only to take note of what is happening before their eyes and
to become its mouthpiece. So long as they look for science and
merely make systems, so long as they are at the beginning of the
struggle, they see in poverty nothing but poverty, without seeing
in it the revolutionary, subversive side, which will overthrow the
old society. From this moment, science, which is a product of the
historical movement, has associated itself consciously with it,
has ceased to be doctrinaire and has become revolutionary.

Let us return to M. Proudhon.

Every economic relation has a good and a bad side; it is the
one point on which M. Proudhon does not give himself the lie. He
sees the good side expounded by the economists; the bad side he
sees denounced by the Socialists. He borrows from the economists the necessity of eternal relations; he borrows from the
Socialists the illusion of seeing in poverty nothing but poverty.
He is in agreement with both in wanting to fall back upon the
authority of science. Science for him reduces itself to the slender
proportions of a scientific formula; he is the man in search of
formulas. Thus it is that M. Proudhon flatters himself on having
given a criticism of both political economy and communism: he is
beneath them both. Beneath the economists, since, as a philosopher who has at his elbow a magic formula, he thought he could
dispense with going into purely economic details; beneath the

Socialists, because he has neither courage enough nor insight enough to rise, be it even speculatively, above the bourgeois horizon.

He wants to be the synthesis—he is a composite error.

He wants to soar as the man of science above the bourgeois and the proletarians; he is merely the petty bourgeois, continually tossed back and forth between capital and labour, political economy and communism.

§2. DIVISION OF LABOUR AND MACHINERY

The division of labour, according to M. Proudhon, opens the series of *economic evolutions.*

Good side of the division of labour

"Considered in its essence, the division of labour is the manner in which *equality of* conditions and intelligence is realized." (Vol. I, p. 93.)

"The division of labour has become for us an instrument of poverty." (Vol. I, p. 94.)

Variant

Bad side of the division of labour

"Labour, by *dividing itself according to the law* which is peculiar to it, and which is the primary condition of its fruitfulness, ends in the negation of its aims and destroys itself." (Vol. I, p. 94.)

Problem to be solved

To find the "recomposition which wipes out the drawbacks of the division, while retaining its useful effects." (Vol. I, p. 97.)

The division of labour is, according to M. Proudhon, an eternal law, a simple, abstract category. Therefore the abstraction, the idea, the word must suffice for him to explain the division of labour at different historical epochs. Castes, corporations, manufacture, large-scale industry must be explained by the single word *divide.* First study carefully the meaning of "divide," and you will have no need to study the numerous influences which give the division of labour a definite character in every epoch.

Certainly, things would be made much too easy if they were reduced to M. Proudhon's categories. History does not proceed so categorically. It took three whole centuries in Germany to establish the first big division of labour, the separation of the towns from the country. In proportion as this one relation of town and country was modified, the whole of society was modified. To take only this one aspect of the division of labour, you have the old republics, and you have Christian feudalism; you have old England with its barons and you have modern England with its cotton lords. In the fourteenth and fifteenth centuries, when there were as yet no colonies, when America did not yet exist for Europe, when Asia existed only through the intermediary of Constantinople, when the Mediterranean was the centre of commercial activity, the division of labour had a very different form, a very different aspect from that of the seventeenth century, when the Spanish, the Portuguese, the Dutch, the English, and the French had colonies established in all parts of the world. The extent of the market, its physiognomy, give to the division of labour at different periods a physiognomy, a character, which it would be difficult to deduce from the single word *divide,* from the idea, from the category.

> "All economists since Adam Smith," says M. Proudhon, "have pointed out the *advantages and drawbacks* of the law of division, but insist -much more on the first than on the second, because that was more serviceable for their optimism, and none of them has ever wondered what could be the drawbacks to a law.... How does the same principle, pursued vigorously to its consequences, lead to diametrically opposite results? Not one economist before or since A. Smith has even perceived that here was a problem to elucidate. Say goes to the length of recognizing that in the division of labour the same cause that produces the good engenders the bad." [I: 95-96]

Adam Smith goes further than M. Proudhon thinks. He saw clearly that "the difference of natural talents in different men is, in reality, much less than we are aware of; and the very different genius which appears to distinguish men of different professions, when grown up to maturity, is not so much the *cause* as the *effect* of the division of labour" [I: 20].[29] In principle, a porter differs less from a philosopher than a mastiff from a greyhound. It is the division of labour which has set a gulf between them. All this does not prevent M. Proudhon from saying elsewhere that Adam Smith had not the slightest idea of the drawbacks produced by the division of labour. It is this again that makes him say that J. B. Say was the *first* to recognize "that in the division of labour the same cause that produces the good engenders the bad." [I: 96]

But let us listen to Lemontey; *Suum cuique.**

> M. J. B. Say has done me the honour of adopting in his excellent treatise on political economy the principle *that I brought to light* in this fragment on the moral influence of the division of labour. The somewhat frivolous title of my book[30] doubtless prevented him from citing me. It is only to this motive that I can attribute the silence of a writer too rich in his own stock to disavow so modest a loan. (Lemontey, *CEuvres complètes*, Vol. I, p. 245, Paris, 1840.)

Let us do him this justice: Lemontey wittily exposed the unpleasant consequences of the division of labour as it is constituted today, and M. Proudhon found nothing to add to it. But now that, through the fault of M. Proudhon, we have been drawn into this question of priority, let us say again, in passing, that long before M. Lemontey, and seventeen years before Adam Smith, who was a pupil of A. Ferguson, the last-named gave a clear exposition of the subject in a chapter which deals specifically with the division of labour.

> It may even be doubted, whether the measure of national capacity increases with the advancement of arts. Many mechanical arts ... succeed best under a total suppression of sentiment and reason; and ignorance is the mother of industry as well as of superstition. Reflection and fancy are subject to err; but a habit of moving the hand, or the foot, is independent of either. Manufactures, accordingly, prosper most, where the mind is least consulted, and where the workshop may, without any great effort of imagination, be considered as an engine, the parts of which are men.... The general officer may be a great proficient in the knowledge of war, while the skill of the soldier is confined to a few motions of the hand and the foot. The former may have gained what the latter has lost.... And thinking itself, in this age of separations, may become a peculiar craft. (A. Ferguson, *An Essay on the History of Civil Society*, Edinburgh 1783 [II: 108, 109, 110].)

To bring this literary survey to a close, we expressly deny that "*all* economists have insisted far more on the advantages than on the drawbacks of the division of labour." It suffices to mention Sismondi.

Thus, as far as the *advantages* of the division of labour are concerned, M. Proudhon had nothing further to do than to paraphrase the general phrases known to everybody.

Let us now see how he derives from the division of labour, taken as a general law, as a category, as a thought, the *drawbacks* which are attached to it. How is it that this category, this

---

* To each one his own.

law implies an unequal distribution of labour to the detriment of
M. Proudhon's equalitarian system?

> At this solemn hour of the division of labour, the storm winds begin to blow
> over humanity. Progress does not take place for all in an equal and uniform
> manner.... It begins by taking possession of a small number of the privi-
> leged.... It is this preference for persons on the part of progress that has for
> so long kept up the belief in the natural and providential inequality of
> conditions, has given rise to castes, and hierarchically constituted all
> societies. (Proudhon, Vol. I, p. 94.)

The division of labour created castes. Now, castes are the drawbacks of the division of labour; thus it is the division of labour that has
engendered the drawbacks. *Quod erat demonstrandum.** Will you go
further and ask what made the division of labour create castes, hierar-
chical constitutions and privileged persons? M. Proudhon will tell you:
Progress. And what made progress? Limitation. Limitation, for M.
Proudhon, is acceptance of persons on the part of progress.

After philosophy comes history. It is no longer either descriptive
history or dialectical history, it is comparative history. M. Proudhon
establishes a parallel between the present-day printing worker and
the printing worker of the Middle Ages; between the worker of
Creusot[31] and the country blacksmith; between the man of letters
of today and the man of letters of the Middle Ages, and he weighs
down the balance on the side of those who belong more or less to
the division of labour as the Middle Ages constituted or transmitted
it. He opposes the division of labour of one historical epoch to the
division of labour of another historical epoch. Was that what M.
Proudhon had to prove? No. He should have shown us the drawbacks of the division of labour in general, of the division of labour as
a category. Besides, why stress this part of M. Proudhon's work,
since a little later we shall see him formally retract all these alleged
developments? Continues M. Proudhon:

> The first effect of fractional labour, after the *deprivation of the soul,* is the
> prolongation of the shifts, which grow in inverse ratio to the sum total of
> intelligence expended.... But as the length of the shifts cannot exceed
> sixteen to eighteen hours per day, the moment the compensation cannot be
> taken out of the time, it will be taken out of the price, and the wages will
> diminish.... What is certain, and the only thing for us to note, is that the
> *universal conscience* does not assess at the same rate the work of a foreman
> and the labour of a mechanic's assistant. It is *therefore* necessary to reduce
> the price of the day's work; so that the worker, after having been afflicted
> in his soul by a degrading function, cannot escape being struck in his body
> by the meagreness of his remuneration. [I: 97-98]

---

* Which was the thing to be proved.

We pass over the logical value of these syllogisms, which Kant would call paralogisms which lead astray.

This is the substance of it:

The division of labour reduces the worker to a degrading function; to this degrading function corresponds a depraved soul; to the depravation of the soul is befitting an ever-increasing wage reduction. And to prove that this reduction is befitting to a depraved soul, M. Proudhon says, to relieve his conscience, that the universal conscience wills it thus. Is M. Proudhon's soul to be reckoned as a part of the universal conscience?

Machinery is, for M. Proudhon, "the logical antithesis of the division of labour," and with the help of his dialectics, he begins by transforming machinery into *the workshop.*

After presupposing the modern workshop, in order to make poverty the outcome of the division of labour, M. Proudhon presupposes poverty engendered by the division of labour, in order to come to the workshop and be able to represent it as the dialectical negation of that poverty. After striking the worker morally by a *degrading function,* physically by the meagreness of the wage; after putting the worker under the *dependence of the foreman,* and debasing his work to the *labour of a mechanic's assistant,* he lays the blame again on the workshop and the machinery for *degrading* the worker "by giving him a *master,*" and he completes his abasement by making him "sink from the rank of artisan to that of common *labourer.*" Excellent dialectics! And if he only stopped there! But no, he has to have a new history of the division of labour, not any longer to derive the contradictions from it, but to reconstruct the workshop after his own fashion. To attain this end he finds himself compelled to forget all he has just said about division.

Labour is organized, is divided differently according to the instruments it disposes over. The hand-mill presupposes a different division of labour from the steam-mill. Thus it is slapping history in the face to want to begin by the division of labour in general, in order to get subsequently to a specific instrument of production, machinery.

Machinery is no more an economic category than the bullock that drags the plough. Machinery is merely a productive force. The modern workshop, which depends on the application of machinery, is a social production relation, an economic category.

Let us see now how things happen in M. Proudhon's brilliant imagination.

In society, the incessant appearance of machinery is the antithesis, the inverse formula of the division of labour: it is the *protest* of the industrial genius against *fractional and homicidal labour.* What, actually, is a machine? *A way of uniting different portions of labour* which had been separated by the division of labour. Every machine can be defined as a summary of several operations.... Thus through the machine there will be *a restoration of the worker*.... Machinery, which in political economy places itself in contradiction to the division of labour, represents synthesis, which in the human mind is opposed to analysis.... Division merely separated the different parts of labour, letting each one devote himself to the speciality which most suited him; the workshop groups the workers according to the relation of each part to the whole.... It introduces the principle of authority in labour.... But this is not all; *the machine* or the *workshop,* after degrading the worker by giving him a master, completes his abasement by making him sink from the rank of artisan to that of common labourer.... The period we are going through at the moment, that of machinery, is distinguished by a special characteristic, the *wage worker*. The wage worker is *subsequent* to the division of labour and to exchange. [I: 135, 136, 161]

Just a simple remark to M. Proudhon. The separation of the different parts of labour, leaving to each one the opportunity of devoting himself to the speciality best suited to him—a separation which M. Proudhon dates from the beginning of the world—exists only in modern industry under the rule of competition.

M. Proudhon goes on to give us a most "interesting genealogy," to show how the workshop arose from the division of labour and the wage worker from the workshop.

1) He supposes a man who "noticed that by dividing up production into its different parts and having each one performed by a separate worker," the forces of production would be-multiplied.

2) This man, "grasping the thread of this idea, tells himself that, by forming a permanent group of workers selected for the special purpose he *sets himself,* he will obtain a more sustained production, etc." [I: 161]

3) This man makes a *proposal* to other men, to make them grasp his idea and the thread of his idea.

4) This man, at the beginning of industry, deals on *terms of equality with his companions* who later become *his workmen.*

5) One realizes, in fact, that this original equality had rapidly to disappear in view of the advantageous position of the master and the dependence of the wage-earner." [I: 163]

That is another example of M. Proudhon's *historical and descriptive method.*

Let us now examine, from the historical and economic point of view, whether the workshop or the machine really introduced the *principle of authority* in society subsequently to the division of labour; whether it rehabilitated the worker on the one hand, while submitting him to authority on the other; whether the machine is the recomposition of divided labour, the *synthesis* of labour as opposed to its *analysis.*

Society as a whole has this in common with the interior of a workshop, that it too has its division of labour. If one took as a model the division of labour in a modern workshop, in order to apply it to a whole society, the society best organized for the production of wealth would undoubtedly be that which had a single chief employer, distributing tasks to the different members of the community according to a previously fixed rule. But this is by no means the case. While inside the modern workshop the division of labour is meticulously regulated by the authority of the employer, modern society has no other rule, no other authority for the distribution of labour than free competition.

Under the patriarchal system, under the caste system, under the feudal and corporative system, there was division of labour in the whole of society according to fixed rules. Were these rules established by a legislator? No. Originally born of the conditions of material production, they were raised to the status of laws only much later. In this way these different forms of the division of labour became so many bases of social organization. As for the division of labour in the workshop, it was very little developed in all these forms of society.

It can even be laid down as a general rule that the less authority presides over the division of labour inside society, the more the division of labour develops inside the workshop, and the more it is subjected there to the authority of a single person. Thus authority in the workshop and authority in society, in relation to the division of labour, are in *inverse ratio* to each other.

The question now is what kind of workshop it is in which the occupations are very much separated, where each worker's task is reduced to a very simple operation, and where the authority, capital, groups and directs the work. How was this workshop brought into existence? In order to answer this question we shall have to examine how manufacturing industry, properly so-called, has developed. I am speaking here of that industry which is not yet modern industry, with its machinery, but which is already no longer the industry of the artisans of the Middle Ages, nor domestic industry. We shall not go into great detail: we shall merely give a few main points to show that history is not to be made with formulas.

One of the most indispensable conditions for the formation of manufacturing industry was the accumulation of capital, facilitated by the discovery of America and the import of its precious metals.

It is sufficiently proved that the increase in the means of exchange resulted in the depreciation of wages and land rents, on the one hand, and the growth of industrial profits on the other. In other words: to the Extent that the propertied class and the working class, the feudal lords and the people, sank, to that extent the capitalist class, the bourgeoisie, rose.

There were yet other circumstances which contributed simultaneously to the development of manufacturing industry: the increase of commodities put into circulation from the moment that trade had penetrated to the East Indies by way of the Cape of Good Hope; the colonial system; the development of maritime trade.

Another point which has not yet been sufficiently appreciated in the history of manufacturing industry is the disbanding of the numerous retinues of feudal lords, whose subordinate ranks became vagrants before entering the workshop. The creation of the workshop was preceded by an almost universal vagrancy in the fifteenth and sixteenth centuries. The workshop found, besides, a powerful support in the many peasants who, continually driven from the country owing to the transformation of the fields into pastures and to the progress in agriculture which necessitated fewer hands for the tillage of the soil, went on congregating in the towns during whole centuries.

The growth of the market, the accumulation of capital, the modification in the social position of the classes, a large number of persons being deprived of their sources of income, all these are historical preconditions for the formation of manufacture. It was not, as M. Proudhon says, friendly agreements between equals that brought men together into the workshop. It was not even in the bosom of the old guilds that manufacture was born. It was the merchant that became the head of the modern workshop, and not the old guild-master. Almost everywhere there was a desperate struggle between manufacture and crafts.

The accumulation and concentration of instruments and workers preceded the development of the division of labour inside the workshop. Manufacture consisted much more in the bringing together of many workers and many crafts in one place, in one room under the command of one capital, than in the analysis of labour and the adaptation of a special worker to a very simple task.

The utility of a workshop consisted much less in the division of labour as such than in the circumstance that work was done on a much larger scale, that many unnecessary, expenses were saved, etc. At the end of the sixteenth and at the beginning of the seventeenth century, Dutch manufacture scarcely knew any division of labour.

The development of the division of labour supposes the assemblage of workers in a workshop. There is not one single example, whether in the sixteenth or in the seventeenth century, of the different branches of one and the same craft being exploited separately to such an extent that it would have sufficed to assemble them all in one place so as to obtain a complete, ready-made workshop. But once the men and the instruments had been brought together, the division of labour, such as it had existed in the form of the guilds, was reproduced, necessarily reflected inside the workshop.

For M. Proudhon, who sees things upside down, if he sees them at all, the division of labour, in Adam Smith's sense, precedes the workshop, which is a condition of its existence.

Machinery, properly so-called, dates from the end of the eighteenth century. Nothing is more absurd than to see in machinery the *antithesis* of the division of labour, the *synthesis* restoring unity to divided labour.

The machine is a unification of the instruments of labour, and by no means a combination of different operations for the worker himself. "When, by the division of labour, each particular operation has been simplified to the use of a single instrument, the linking-up of all these instruments, set in motion by a single engine, constitutes—a machine."[32] Simple tools; accumulation of tools; composite tools; setting in motion of a composite tool by a single hand engine, by man; setting in motion of these instruments by natural forces, machines; system of machines having one motor; system of machines having one automatic motor-this is the progress of machinery.

The concentration of the instruments of production and the division of labour are as inseparable one from the other as are, in the political sphere, the concentration of public authority and the division of private interests. England, with the concentration of the land. this instrument of agricultural labour, has at the same time division of agricultural labour and the application of machinery to the exploitation of the soil. France, which has the division of the instruments, the small holdings system, has, in general, neither division of agricultural labour nor application of machinery to the soil.

For M. Proudhon the concentration of the instruments of labour is the negation of the division of labour. In reality we find again the reverse. As the concentration of instruments develops, the division develops also, and *vice versa*. This is why every big mechanical invention is followed by a greater division of labour, and each increase in the division of labour gives rise in turn to new mechanical inventions.

We need not recall the fact that the great progress of the division of labour began in England after the invention of machinery. Thus the weavers and spinners were for the most part peasants like those one still meets in backward countries. The invention of machinery brought about the separation of manufacturing industry from agricultural industry. The weaver and the spinner, united but lately in a single family, were separated by the machine. Thanks to the machine, the spinner can live in England while the weaver resides in the East Indies. Before the invention of machinery, the industry of a country was carried on chiefly with raw materials that were the products of its own soil; in England—wool, in Germany—flax, in France—silks and flax, in the East Indies and the Levant—cotton, etc. Thanks to the application of machinery and of steam, the division of labour was able to assume such dimensions that large-scale industry, detached from the national soil, depends entirely on the world market, on international exchange, on an international division of labour. In short—the machine has so great an influence on the division of labour, that when, in the manufacture of some object, a means has been found to produce parts of it mechanically, the manufacture splits up immediately into two works independent of each other.

Need we speak of the philanthropic and *providential* aim that M. Proudhon discovers in the invention and first application of machinery?

When in England the market had become so far developed that manual labour was no longer adequate, the need for machinery was felt. Then came the idea of the application of mechanical science, already quite developed -in the eighteenth century.

The automatic workshop opened its career with acts which were anything but philanthropic. Children were kept at work at the whip's end; they were made an object of traffic and contracts were undertaken with the orphanages. All the laws on the apprenticeship of workers were repealed, because, to use M. Proudhon's phraseology, there was no further need of *synthetic* workers. Finally, from 1825 onwards,[33] almost all the new inventions were the result of collisions between the worker and the employer who sought at all costs to depreciate the worker's specialized ability. After each new strike of any importance, there appeared a new machine. So little indeed did the worker see in the application of machinery a sort of rehabilitation, *restoration*—as M. Proudhon would say—that in the eighteenth century he stood out for a very long time against the incipient domination of the automaton.

"Wyatt," says Doctor Ure, "invented the series of fluted rollers ... (the spinning fingers usually ascribed to Arkwright)...."

> The main difficulty did not, to my apprehension, lie so much in the invention of a proper self-acting mechanism ... as in training human beings to renounce their desultory habits of work, and to identify themselves with the unvarying regularity of the complex automaton. But to devise and administer a successful code of factory discipline, suited to the necessities of factory diligence, was the Herculean enterprise, the noble achievement of Arkwright. [I: 21-22, 23]

In short, by the introduction of machinery the division of labour inside society has grown up, the task of the worker inside the workshop has been simplified, capital has been concentrated, human beings have been further dismembered.

When M. Proudhon wants to be an economist, and to abandon for a moment the "evolution of ideas in serial relation in the understanding," then he goes and draws erudition from Adam Smith, from a time when the automatic workshop was only just coming into existence. Indeed, what a difference between the division of labour as it existed in Adam Smith's day and as we see it in the automatic workshop! In order to make this properly understood, we need only quote a few passages from Dr. Ure's *The Philosophy of Manufactures*.*

> When Adam Smith wrote his immortal elements of economics, automatic machinery being hardly known, he was properly led to regard the division of labour as the grand principle of manufacturing improvement; and he showed, in the example of pin-making, how each handicraftsman, being thereby enabled to perfect himself by practice in one point, became a quicker and cheaper workman. In each branch of manufacture he saw that some parts were, on that principle, of easy execution, like the cutting of pin wires into uniform lengths, and some were comparatively difficult, like the formation and fixation of their heads; and therefore he concluded that to each a workman of appropriate value and cost was naturally assigned. This *appropriation* forms the very essence of the division of labour.... But what was in Dr. Smith's time a topic of useful illustration, cannot now be used without risk of misleading the public mind as to the right principle of manufacturing industry. In fact, the division, or rather adaptation of labour to the different talents of men, is little thought of in factory employment. On the contrary, wherever a process requires peculiar dexterity and steadiness of hand, it is withdrawn as soon as possible from the cunning workman, who is prone to irregularities of many kinds, and it is placed in charge of a peculiar mechanism, so self-regulating, that a child may superintend it.

* A. Ure, *Philosophie des manufactures*, t. I, Bruxelles, 1836, pp. 23, 21, 22.

The principle of the factory system then is, to substitute mechanical science for hand skill, and the partition of a process into its essential constituents, for the division or gradation of labour among artisans. On the handicraft plan, labour more or less skilled, was usually the most expensive element of production ... but on the automatic plan, skilled labour gets progressively superseded, and will, eventually, be replaced by mere overlookers of machines.

By the infirmity of human nature it happens, that the more skillful the workman, the more self-willed and intractable he is apt tor become, and, of course, the less fit a component of a mechanical system, in which, by occasional irregularities, he may do great damage to the whole. The grand object therefore of the modern manufacture is, through the union of capital and science, to reduce the task of his workpeople to the exercise of vigilance and dexterity—faculties, *when concentrated to one process,* speedily brought to perfection in the young.

On the gradation system, a man must serve an apprenticeship of many years before his hand and eve become skilled enough for certain mechanical feats; but on the system of decomposing a process into its constituents, and embodying each part in an automatic machine, a person of common care and capacity may be entrusted with any of the said elementary parts after a short probation, and may be transferred from one to another, on any emergency, at the discretion of the master. Such translations are utterly at variance with the old practice of the division of labour, which fixed one man to shaping the head of a pin, and another to sharpening its point, with most irksome and spirit-wasting uniformity, for a whole life.... But on *the equalization* plan of self-acting machines, the operative needs to call his faculties only into agreeable exercise.... As his business consists in tending the work of a well-regulated mechanism, he can learn it in a short period; and when he transfers his services from one machine to another, he varies his task, and enlarges his views, by thinking on those general combinations which result from his and his companions' labours. Thus, that cramping of the faculties, that narrowing of the mind, that stunting of the frame, which were ascribed, and not unjustly, by moral writers, to the division of labour, cannot, in common circumstances, occur under the *equable distribution of industry....*

It is, in fact, the constant aim and tendency of every improvement in machinery to supersede human labour altogether, or to diminish its cost, by substituting the industry of women and children for that of men; or that of ordinary labourers for trained artisans.... This tendency to employ merely children with watchful eyes and nimble fingers, instead of journeymen of long experience, shows how the scholastic dogma of the division of labour into degrees of skill has been exploded by our enlightened manufacturers. (André Ure, *Philosophie des manufactures ou Économie industrielle,* Vol. I, Chap. 1 [pp. 34-35].)

What characterizes the division of labour inside modern society is that it engenders specialized functions, specialists, and with them craft-idiocy. Says Lemontey:

We are struck with admiration, when we see among the Ancients the same person distinguishing himself to a high degree as philosopher, poet, orator, historian, priest, administrator, general of an army. Our souls are appalled at the sight of so vast a domain. Each one of us plants his hedge and shuts himself up in his enclosure. I do not know whether by this parcellation the field is enlarged, but I do know that man is belittled (p. 213)

What characterizes the division of labour in the automatic workshop is that labour has there completely lost its specialized character. But the moment every special development stops, the need for universality, the tendency towards an integral development of the individual begins to be felt. The automatic workshop wipes out specialists and craft-idiocy.

M. Proudhon, not having understood even this one revolutionary side of the automatic workshop, takes a step backward and proposes to the worker that he make not only the twelfth part of a pin, but successively all twelve parts of it. The worker would thus arrive at the knowledge and the consciousness of the pin. This is M. Proudhon's synthetic labour. Nobody will contest that to make a movement forward and another movement backward is also to make a synthetic movement.

To sum up, M. Proudhon has not gone further than the petty-bourgeois ideal. And to realize this ideal, he can think of nothing better than to take us back to the journeyman or, at most, to the master craftsman of the Middle Ages. It is enough, he says somewhere in his book, to have created a masterpiece once in one's life, to have felt oneself just once to be a man. Is not this, in form as in content, the masterpiece demanded by the trade guild of the Middle Ages.

§3. COMPETITION AND MONOPOLY

Good side of competition

"Competition is as essential to labour as division.... It is necessary for the *advent of equality.*" [I: 186, 188]

Bad side of competition

"The principle is the negation of itself. Its most certain result is to ruin those whom it drags in its train." [I: 185]

General reflection

"*The drawbacks* which follow in its wake, just as the good it provides ... both flow logically from the principle." [I: 185-186]

<table>
<tr><td>

Problem to be solved

</td><td>

"To seek the principle of *accommodation*, which must be derived from a law superior to liberty itself." [I: 185]

Variant

"There can, therefore, be no question here of destroying competition, a thing as impossible to destroy as liberty; we have only to find its equilibrium, I would be ready to say its police." [I: 223]

</td></tr>
</table>

M. Proudhon begins by defending the eternal necessity of competition against those who wish to replace it by emulation.*

> There is no "purposeless emulation," and as "the object of every passion is necessarily analogous to the passion itself—a woman for the lover, power for the ambitious, gold for the miser, a garland for the poet—the object of industrial emulation is necessarily profit. Emulation is nothing but competition itself." [I: 187]

Competition is emulation with a view to profit. Is industrial emulation necessarily emulation with a view to profit, that is, competition? M. Proudhon proves it by affirming it. We have seen that, for him, to affirm is to prove, just as to suppose is to deny.

If the immediate object of the lover is the woman, the immediate object of industrial emulation is the product and not the profit.

Competition is not industrial emulation, it is commercial emulation. In our time industrial emulation exists only in view of commerce. There are even phases in the economic life of modern nations when everybody is seized with a sort of craze for making profit without producing. This speculation craze, which recurs periodically, lays bare the true character of competition, which seeks to escape the need for industrial emulation.

If you had told an artisan of the fourteenth century that the privileges and the whole feudal organization of industry were going to be abrogated in favour of industrial emulation, called competition, he would have replied that the privileges of the various corporations, guilds and fraternities were organized competition. M. Proudhon does not improve upon this when he affirms that "emulation is nothing but competition itself."

---

* The Fourierists. [Note by Engels to the German edition of 1885.]

"Decree that from the first of January, 1847, labour and wages shall be guaranteed to everybody: immediately an immense relaxation will succeed the high tension of industry." [I: 189]

Instead of a supposition, an affirmation and a negation, we have now a decree that M. Proudhon issues purposely to prove the necessity of competition, its eternity as a category, etc.

If we imagine that decrees are all that is needed to get away from competition, we shall never get away from it. And if we go so far as to propose to abolish competition while retaining wages, we shall be proposing nonsense by royal decree. But nations do not proceed by royal decree. Before framing such ordinances, they must at least have changed from top to bottom the conditions of their industrial and political existence, and consequently their whole manner of being.

M. Proudhon will reply, with his imperturbable assurance, that it is the hypothesis of "a transformation of our nature without historical antecedents," and that he would be right in *"excluding* us from the discussion,"* we know not in virtue of which ordinance.

M. Proudhon does not know that all history is nothing but a continuous transformation of human nature.

Let us stick to the facts. The French Revolution was made for industrial liberty as much as for political liberty; and although France, in 1789, had not perceived—let us say it openly—all the consequences of the principle whose realization it demanded, it was mistaken neither in its wishes nor in its expectations. Whoever attempts to deny this loses, in my view, the right to criticism. I will never dispute with an adversary who puts as principle the spontaneous error of twenty-five million men.... Why then, if competition had not been a *principle* of social economy, a *decree of fate, a necessity of the human soul,* why, instead of *abolishing* corporations, guilds and brotherhoods, did nobody think rather of *repairing* the whole?" [I: 191, 192]

So, since the French of the eighteenth century abolished corporations, guilds and fraternities instead of modifying them, the French of the nineteenth century must modify competition instead of abolishing it. Since competition was established in France in the eighteenth century as a result of historical needs, this competition must not be destroyed in the nineteenth century because of other historical needs. M. Proudhon, not understanding that the establishment of competition was bound up with the actual development of the men of the eighteenth century, makes of competition a necessity of the *human soul, in partibus infidelium.*[34] What would he have made of the great Colbert for the seventeenth century?

After the revolution comes the present state of affairs. M. Proudhon equally draws facts from it to show the eternity of

competition, by proving that all industries in which this category
is not yet sufficiently developed, as in agriculture, are in a state
of inferiority and decrepitude.

To say that there are industries which have not yet reached
the stage of competition, that others again are below the level of
bourgeois production, is drivel which gives not the slightest proof
of the eternity of competition.

All M. Proudhon's logic amounts to this: competition is a social
relation in which we are now developing our productive forces.
To this truth, he gives no logical development, but only forms,
often very well developed, when he says that competition is industrial emulation, the present-day mode of freedom, responsibility in labour, constitution of value, a condition for the advent
of equality, a principle of social economy, a decree of fate, a
necessity of the human soul, an inspiration of eternal justice,
liberty in division, division in liberty, an economic category.

> *Competition and association* support each other. Far from excluding each
> other they are not even *divergent.* Whoever says competition already
> supposes a *common* aim. Competition is therefore not *egoism,* and the most
> deplorable error committed by socialism is to have regarded it as the
> overthrow of society. [I: 223]

Whoever says competition says common aim, and that proves,
on the one hand, that competition is association; on the other,
that competition is not egoism. And whoever says *egoism,* does
he not say common aim? Every egoism operates in society and by
the fact of society. Hence it presupposes society, that is to say,
common aims, common needs, common means of production, etc.,
etc. Is it, then, by mere chance that the competition and association which the Socialists talk about are not even divergent?

Socialists know well enough that present-day society is
founded on competition. How could they accuse competition of
overthrowing present-day society which they want to overthrow
themselves? And how could they accuse competition of overthrowing the society to come, in which they see, on the contrary,
the overthrow of competition?

M. Proudhon says, later on, that competition is the *opposite of
monopoly,* and consequently cannot be the *opposite of association.*

Feudalism was, from its origin, opposed to patriarchal monarchy; it was thus not opposed to competition, which was not yet
in existence. Does it follow that competition is not opposed to
feudalism?

In actual fact, *society, association* are denominations which
can be given to every society, to feudal society as well as to

bourgeois society, which is association founded on competition. How then can there be Socialists, who, by the single word *association*, think they can refute competition? And how can M. Proudhon himself wish to defend competition against socialism by describing competition by the single word *association?*

All we have just said makes up the beautiful side of competition as M. Proudhon sees it. Now let us pass on to the ugly side, that is the negative side, of competition, its drawbacks, its destructive, subversive elements, its injurious qualities.

There is something dismal about the picture M. Proudhon draws of it.

Competition engenders misery, it foments civil war, it "changes natural zones," mixes up nationalities, causes trouble in families, corrupts the public conscience, "subverts the notion of equity, of justice," of morality, and what is worse, it destroys free, honest trade, and does not even give in exchange *synthetic value*, fixed, honest price. It disillusions everyone, even economists. It pushes things so far as to destroy its very self.

After all the ill M. Proudhon says of it, can there be for the relations of bourgeois society, for its principles and its illusions, a more disintegrating, more destructive element than competition?

It must be carefully noted that competition always becomes the more destructive for bourgeois *relations* in proportion as it urges on a feverish creation of new productive forces, that is, of the material conditions of a new society. In this respect at least, the bad side of competition would have its good points.

"Competition as an economic position or phase, considered in its origin, is the necessary result ... of the theory of the reduction of general expenses." [I: 235] For M. Proudhon, the circulation of the blood must be a consequence of Harvey's theory.

"*Monopoly* is the inevitable end of competition, which engenders it by a continual negation of itself. This generation of monopoly is in itself a justification of it.... Monopoly is the natural opposite of competition ... but as soon as competition is necessary, it implies the idea of monopoly, since monopoly is, as it were, the seat of each competing individuality." [I: 236, 237]

We rejoice with M. Proudhon that he can for once at least properly apply his formula to thesis and antithesis. Everyone knows that modern monopoly is engendered by competition itself.

As for the content, M. Proudhon clings to poetic images. Competition made "of every subdivision of labour a sort of sovereignty in which each individual stood with his power and his independence." Monopoly is "the *seat* of every competing individuality." The sovereignty is worth at least as much as the seat.

M. Proudhon talks of nothing but modern monopoly engendered by competition. But we all know that competition was engendered by feudal monopoly. Thus competition was originally the opposite of monopoly and not monopoly the opposite of competition. So that modern monopoly is not a simple antithesis, it is on the contrary the true synthesis.

Thesis: Feudal monopoly, before competition.

Antithesis: Competition.

Synthesis: Modern monopoly, which is the negation of feudal monopoly, in so far as it implies the system of competition, and the negation of competition in so far as it is monopoly.

Thus modern monopoly, bourgeois monopoly, is synthetic monopoly, the negation of the negation, the unity of opposites. It is monopoly in the pure, normal, rational state.

M. Proudhon is in contradiction with his own philosophy when he turns bourgeois monopoly into monopoly in the crude, *primitive*, contradictory, spasmodic state. M. Rossi, whom M. Proudhon quotes several times on the subject of monopoly, seems to have a better grasp of the synthetic character of bourgeois monopoly. In his *Cours d'économie politique*,[35] he distinguishes between artificial monopolies and natural monopolies. Feudal monopolies, he says, are artificial, that is, arbitrary; bourgeois monopolies are natural, that is, rational.

Monopoly is a good thing, reasons M. Proudhon, since it is an economic category, an emanation "from the impersonal reason of humanity." Competition, again, is a good thing since it also is an economic category. But what is not good is the reality of monopoly and the reality of competition. What is still worse is that competition and monopoly devour each other. What is to be done? Look for the synthesis of these two eternal thoughts, wrest it from the bosom of God, where it has been deposited from time immemorial.

In practical life we find not only competition, monopoly and the antagonism between them, but also the synthesis of the two, which is not a formula, but a movement. Monopoly produces competition, competition produces monopoly. Monopolists are made from competition; competitors become monopolists. If the monopolists restrict their mutual competition by means of partial associations, competition increases among the workers; and the more the mass of the proletarians grows as against the monopolists of one nation, the more desperate competition becomes between the monopolists of different nations. The synthesis is of such a character that monopoly can only maintain itself by continually entering into the struggle of competition.

To make the dialectical transition to the *taxes* which come after *monopoly*, M. Proudhon talks to us about *the social* genius which, after *zigzagging intrepidly onward,*

> after striding with a jaunty step, *without repenting* and without halting, *reaches the corner of monopoly,* casts backward a melancholy glance, and, after profound reflection, assails all the objects of production with taxes, and creates a whole administrative organization, in order that *all employments be given to the proletariat and paid by the men of monopoly.* [I: 284, 285]

What can we say of this genius, which, while fasting, walks about in a zigzag? And what can we say of this walking which has no other object in view than that of destroying the bourgeois by taxes, whereas taxes are the very means of giving the bourgeois the wherewithal to preserve themselves as the ruling class?

Merely to give a glimpse of the manner in which M. Proudhon treats economic details, it suffices to say that, according to him, the *tax on consumption was* established with a view to equality, and to relieve the proletariat.

The tax on consumption has assumed its true development only since the rise of the bourgeoisie. In the hands of industrial capital, that is, of sober and economical wealth, which maintains, reproduces and increases itself by the direct exploitation of labour, the tax on consumption was a means of exploiting the frivolous, gay, prodigal wealth of the fine lords who did nothing but consume. James Steuart clearly developed this original purpose of the tax on consumption in his *Recherches des principes de l'économie politique,*[36] which he published ten years before Adam Smith.

> Under the pure monarchy, the prince seems jealous, as it were, of growing wealth, and therefore imposes taxes upon people who are growing richer,—taxes on production. Under constitutional government they are calculated chiefly to affect those who are growing poorer,—taxes on consumption. Thus the monarch imposes a tax upon industry ... the poll-tax and *taille,* for example, are proportioned to the supposed opulence of everyone liable to them. Everyone is taxed in proportion to the gain he is supposed to make. In constitutional governments, impositions are more generally laid upon consumption. Everyone is taxed according to his expenditure. [II: 190-191][37]

As for the *logical sequence* of taxes, of the balance of trade, of credit—in the understanding of M. Proudhon—we would only remark that the English bourgeoisie, on attaining its political constitution under William of Orange, created all at once a new system of taxes, public credit and the system of protective duties, as soon as it was in a position freely to develop its conditions of existence.

This brief summary will suffice to give the reader a true idea of M. Proudhon's lucubrations on the police or on taxes, the balance of trade, credit, communism and population. We defy the most indulgent criticism to treat these chapters seriously.

§4. PROPERTY OR GROUND RENT

In each historical epoch, property has developed differently and under a set of entirely different social relations. Thus to de ne bourgeois property is nothing else than to give an exposition of all the social relations of bourgeois production.

To try to give a definition of property as of an independent relation, a category apart, an abstract and eternal idea, can be nothing but an illusion of metaphysics or jurisprudence.

M. Proudhon, while seeming to speak of property in general, deals only with *landed property, with ground rent.*

> The origin of rent, as property, is, so to speak, extra-economic: it rests in psychological and moral considerations which are only very distantly connected with the production of wealth. (Vol. II, p. 269.)

So M. Proudhon declares himself incapable of understanding the economic origin of rent and of property. He admits that this incapacity obliges him to resort to psychological and moral considerations, which, indeed, while only distantly connected with the production of wealth, have yet a very close connection with the narrowness of his historical views. M. Proudhon affirms that there is something *mystical and mysterious* about the origin of property. Now, to see mystery in the origin of property—that is, to make a mystery of the relation between production itself and the distribution of the instruments of production—is not this, to use M. Proudhon's language, a renunciation of all claims to economic science? M. Proudhon

> confines himself to recalling that at the seventh epoch of economic evolution—credit—when fiction had caused reality to vanish, and human activity threatened to lose itself in empty space, it had become necessary to *bind man more closely to nature.* Now, rent was the price of this new contract. (Vol. II, p. 265.)

L'homme aux quarante écus[38] foresaw a M. Proudhon of the future: "Mr. Creator, by your leave: everyone is master in his own world; but you will never make me believe that the one we live in is made of glass." In your world, where credit was a means of *losing oneself in empty space,* it is very possible that property became necessary in order to *bind man to nature.* In the world of

real production, where landed property always precedes credit,
M. Proudhon's *horror vacui* could not exist.

The existence of rent once admitted, whatever its origin, it
becomes a subject of mutually antagonistic negotiations between
the farmer and the landed proprietor. What is the ultimate result of these negotiations, in other words, what is the average
amount of rent? This is what M. Proudhon says:

> Ricardo's theory answers this question. In the beginnings of society, when
> man, new to earth, had before him nothing but huge forests, when the
> earth was vast and when industry was beginning to come to life, rent must
> have been nil. Land, as yet unformed by labour, was an object of utility; it
> was not an exchange value, it was common, not social. Little by little, the
> multiplication of families and the progress of agriculture caused the price
> of land to make itself felt. Labour came to give the soil its worth: from this,
> rent came into being. The more fruit a field yielded with the same amount
> of labour, the higher it was valued; hence the tendency of proprietors was
> always to arrogate to themselves the whole amount of the fruits of the soil,
> less the wages of the farmer—that is, less the costs of production. Thus
> property followed on the heels of labour to take from it all the product that
> exceeded the actual expenses. As the proprietor fulfils a mystic duty and
> represents the community as against the *colonus,* the farmer is, by the
> dispensation of Providence, no more than a responsible labourer, who must
> account to society for all he reaps above his legitimate wage.... In essence
> and by destination, then, rent is an instrument of distributive justice, one
> of the thousand means that the genius of economy employs to attain to
> equality. It is an immense land valuation which is carried out contradicto-
> rily by landowners and farmers, without any possible collusion, in a higher
> interest, and whose ultimate result must be to equalize the possession of
> the land between the exploiters of the soil and the industrialists.... It
> needed no less than this magic of property to snatch from the *colonus* the
> surplus of his product which he cannot help regarding as his own and of
> which he considers himself to be exclusively the author. Rent, or rather
> property, has broken down agricultural egoism and created a solidarity
> that no power, no partition of the land could have brought into being.... The
> moral effect of property having been secured, at present what remains to
> be done is to distribute the rent. [II: 270-272]

All this tumult of words may be reduced firstly to this: Ricardo
says that the excess of the price of agricultural products over
their cost of production, including the ordinary profit and interest on the capital, gives the measure of the rent. M. Proudhon
does better. He makes the landowner intervene, like a *Deus ex
machina*,[39] and snatch from the *colonus* all the surplus of his
production over the cost of production. He makes use of the intervention of the landowner to explain property, of the intervention
of the rent-receiver to explain rent. He answers the problem by
formulating the same problem and adding an extra syllable.[40]

Let us note also that in determining rent by the difference in
fertility of the soil, M. Proudhon assigns a new origin to it, since

land, before being assessed according to different degrees of fertility, "was not," in his view, "an exchange value, but was common." What, then, has happened to the fiction about rent having come into being *through the necessity* of bringing back *to the land* man who *was about to lose himself in the infinity of empty space?*

Now let us free Ricardo's doctrine from the providential, allegorical and mystical phrases in which M. Proudhon has been careful to wrap it.

Rent, in the Ricardian sense, is property in land in its bourgeois state; that is, feudal property which has become subject to the conditions of bourgeois production.

We have seen that, according to the Ricardian doctrine, the price of all objects is determined ultimately by the cost of production, including the industrial profit; in other words, by the labour time employed. In manufacturing industry, the price of the product obtained by the minimum of labour regulates the price of all other commodities of the same kind, seeing that the cheapest and most productive instruments of production can be multiplied to infinity arid that competition necessarily gives rise to a market price, that is, a common price for all products of the same kind.

In agricultural industry, on the contrary, it is the price of the product obtained by the greatest amount of labour which regulates the price of all products of the same kind. In the first place, one cannot, as in manufacturing industry, multiply at will the instruments of production possessing the same degree of productivity, that is, plots of land with the same degree of fertility. Then, as population increases, land of an inferior quality begins to be exploited, or new outlays of capital, proportionately less productive than before, are made upon the same plot of land. In both cases a greater amount of labour is expended to obtain a proportionately smaller product. The needs of the population having rendered necessary this increase of labour, the product of the land whose exploitation is the more costly has as certain a sale as has that of a piece of land whose exploitation is cheaper. As competition levels the market price, the product of the better soil will be paid for as dearly as that of the inferior. It is the excess of the price of the products of the better soil over the cost of their production that constitutes rent. If one could always have at one's disposal plots of land of the same degree of fertility; if one could, as in manufacturing industry, have recourse continually to cheaper and more productive machines, or if the subsequent outlays of capital produced as much as the first, then the price of agricultural products would be determined by the price of commodities produced by the best instruments of production, as we have seen with the price of manufactured products. But, from this moment rent would have disappeared also.

For the Ricardian doctrine[41] to be generally true, it is essential that capital should be freely applicable to different branches of industry; that a strongly developed competition among capitalists should have brought profits to an equal level; that the farmer should be no more than an industrial capitalist claiming for the use of his capital on inferior land,[42] a profit equal to that which he would draw from his capital if it were applied in any kind of manufacture; that agricultural exploitation should be subjected to the regime of large-scale industry; and finally, that the landowner himself should aim at nothing beyond the money return.

It may happen, as in Ireland, that rent does not yet exist, although the letting of land has reached an extreme development there. Rent being the excess not only over wages, but also over industrial profit, it cannot exist where the landowner's revenue is nothing but a mere levy on wages.

Thus, far from converting the exploiter of the land, the farmer, into a *simple labourer*, and "snatching from the cultivator the surplus of his product, which he cannot help regarding as his own," rent confronts the landowner, not with the slave, the serf, the payer of tribute, the wage labourer, but with the industrial capitalist.[43]

Once constituted as ground rent, landed property has in its possession only the surplus over production costs, which are determined not only by wages but also by industrial profit. It is therefore from the landowner that ground rent snatched a part of his income. Thus, there was a big lapse of time before the feudal farmer was replaced by the industrial capitalist. In Germany, for example, this transformation began only in the last third of the eighteenth century. It is in England alone that this relation between the industrial capitalist and the landed proprietor has been fully developed.

So long as there was only M. Proudhon's *colonus*, there was no rent. The moment rent exists, the *colonus* is no longer the farmer, but the worker, the farmer's *colonus*. The abasement of the labourer, reduced to the role of a simple worker, day labourer, wage-earner, working for the industrial capitalist; the intervention of the industrial capitalist, exploiting the land like any other factory; the transformation of the landed proprietor from a petty sovereign into a vulgar usurer: these are the different relations expressed by rent.

Rent, in the Ricardian sense, is patriarchal agriculture transformed into commercial industry, industrial capital applied to land, the town bourgeoisie transplanted into the country. Rent, instead of *binding man to nature,* has merely bound the exploitation of the land to competition. Once established as rent, landed property itself is the *result of competition,* since from that time onwards it depends on the market value of agricultural produce. As rent, landed property is mobilized and becomes an article of commerce. Rent is possible only from the moment when the development of urban industry, and the social organization resulting therefrom, force the landowner to aim solely at cash profits, at the monetary relation of his agricultural products—in fact to look upon his landed property only as a machine for coining money. Rent has so completely divorced the landed proprietor from the soil, from nature, that he has no need even to know his estates, as is to be seen in England. As for the farmer, the industrial capitalist and the agricultural worker, they are no more bound to the land they exploit than are the employer and the worker in the factories to the cotton and wool they manufacture; they feel an attachment only for the price of their production, the monetary product. Hence the jeremiads of the reactionary parties, who offer up all their prayers for the return of feudalism, of the good old patriarchal life, of the simple manners and the fine virtues of our forefathers. The subjection of the soil to the laws which dominate all other industries is and always will be the subject of interested condolences. Thus it may be said that rent has become the motive power which has introduced idyll into the movement of history.

Ricardo, after postulating bourgeois production as necessary for determining rent, applies the conception of rent, nevertheless, to the landed property of all ages and all countries. This is an error common to all the economists, who represent the bourgeois relations of production as eternal categories.

From the providential aim of rent—which is, for M. Proudhon, the transformation of the *colonus* into a *responsible worker,* he passes to the equalized reward of rent.

Rent, as we have just seen, is constituted by the *equal price* of the products of lands of *unequal fertility,* so that a hectolitre of corn which has cost ten francs is sold for twenty francs if the cost of production rises to twenty francs upon soil of inferior quality.

So long as necessity forces the purchase of all the agricultural products brought into the market, the market price is determined by the cost of the most expensive product. Thus it is this equalization of price, resulting from competition and not from the different fertilities of the lands, that secures to the owner of the better soil a rent of ten francs for every hectolitre that his tenant sells.

Let us suppose for a moment that the price of corn is determined by the labour-time needed to produce it, and at once the hectolitre of corn obtained from the better soil will sell at ten francs, while the hectolitre of corn obtained on the inferior soil will cost twenty francs. This being admitted, the average market price will be fifteen francs, whereas, according to the law of competition, it is twenty francs. If the average price were fifteen francs, there would be no occasion for any distribution, whether equalized or otherwise, for there would be no rent. Rent exists only when one can sell for twenty francs the hectolitre of corn which has cost the producer ten francs. M. Proudhon supposes equality of the market price, with unequal costs of production in order to arrive at an equalized sharing out of the product of inequality.

We understand such economists as Mill, Cherbuliez, Hilditch and others demanding that rent should be handed over to the state to serve in place of taxes. That is a frank expression of the hatred the industrial capitalist bears towards the landed proprietor, who seems to him a useless thing, an excrescence upon the general body of bourgeois production.

But first to make the price of the hectolitre of corn twenty francs in order then to make a general distribution of the ten francs overcharge levied on the consumer, is indeed enough to make the *social genius* pursue *its zigzag course mournfully-and* knock its head against some *corner*.

Rent becomes, under M. Proudhon's pen,

an immense *land valuation* which is carried out contradictorily by landlords and farmers ... in a higher interest, and whose ultimate result must be to equalize the possession of land between exploiters of the soil and the industrialists. [II: 271]

For any land valuation based upon rent to be of practical value, the conditions of present society must not be departed from.

Now, we have shown that the farm rent paid by the farmer to the landlord expresses the rent with any exactitude only in the countries most advanced in industry and commerce. And even this rent often includes interest paid to the landlord on capital incorporated in the land. The location of the land, the vicinity of towns, and many other circumstances influence the farm rent and modify the ground rent. These peremptory reasons would be enough to prove the inaccuracy of a land valuation based on rent.

On the other hand, rent could not be the invariable index of the degree of fertility of a piece of land, since every moment the modern application of chemistry is changing the nature of the soil, and geological knowledge is just now, in our days, beginning to revolutionize all the old estimates of relative fertility. It is only about twenty years since vast plots in the eastern counties of England were cleared; they had been left uncultivated from the lack of proper comprehension of the relation between the humus and the composition of the sub-soil.

Thus history, far from supplying, in rent, a readymade land valuation, does nothing but change and turn topsy-turvy the land valuations already made.

Finally, fertility is not so natural a quality as might be thought; it is closely bound up with the social relations of the time. A piece of land may be very fertile for corn growing, and yet the market price may decide the cultivator to turn it into an artificial pastureland and thus render it infertile, M. Proudhon has improvised his land valuation, which has not even the value of an ordinary land valuation, only to give substance to the *providentially equalitarian aim* of rent.

"Rent," continues M. Proudhon,

> is the interest paid on a capital which never perishes, namely-land. And as the capital is capable of no increase in matter, but only of an indefinite improvement in its use, it comes about that while the interest or profit on a loan *(mutuum)* tends to diminish continually through abundance of capital, rent tends always to increase through the perfecting of industry, from which results the improvement in the use of the land.... Such, in its essence, is rent. (Vol. II, p. 265.)

This time, M. Proudhon sees in rent all the characteristics of interest, save that it is derived from capital of a specific nature. This capital is land, an eternal capital, "which is capable of no increase in matter, but only of an indefinite improvement in its use." In the progressive advance of civilization, interest has a continual tendency to fall, whilst rent continually tends to rise. Interest falls because of the abundance of capital; rent rises owing to the improvements brought about in industry, which result in an ever better utilization of land.

Such, in its essence, is the opinion of M. Proudhon.

Let us first examine how far it is true to say that rent is interest on capital.

For the landed proprietor himself rent represents the interest on the capital that the land has cost him, or that he would draw from it if he sold it. But in buying or selling land he only buys or sells rent. The price he pays to make himself a receiver of rent is regulated by the rate of interest in general and has nothing to do with the actual nature of rent. The interest on capital invested in land is in general lower than the interest on capital invested in manufacture or commerce. Thus, for those who make no distinction between the interest that the land represents to the owner and the rent itself, the interest on land capital diminishes still more than does the interest on other capital. But it is not a question of the purchase or sale price of rent, of the marketable value of rent, of capitalized rent, it is a question of rent itself.

Farm rent can imply again, apart from rent proper, the interest on the capital incorporated in the land. In this instance the landlord receives this part of the farm rent, not as a landlord but as a capitalist; but this is not the rent proper that we are to deal with.

Land, so long as it is not exploited as a means of production, is not capital. Land as capital can be increased just as much as all the other instruments of production. Nothing is added to its matter, to use M. Proudhon's language, but the lands which serve as instruments of production are multiplied. The very fact of applying further outlays of capital to land already transformed into means of production increases land as capital without adding anything to land as matter, that is, to the extent of the land. M. Proudhon's land as matter is the earth in its limitation. As for the eternity he attributes to land, we grant readily it has this virtue as matter. Land as capital is no more eternal than any other capital.

Gold and silver, which yield interest, are just as lasting and eternal as land. If the price of gold and silver falls, while that of land keeps rising, this is certainly not because of its more or less eternal nature.

Land as capital is fixed capital; but fixed capital gets used up just as much as circulating capital. Improvements to the land need reproduction and upkeep; they last only for a time; and this they have in common with all other improvements used to transform matter into means of production. If land as capital were eternal, some lands would present a very different appearance from what they do today, and we should see the Roman Campagna, Sicily, Palestine, in all the splendour of their former prosperity.

There are even instances when land as capital might disappear, even though the improvements remain incorporated in the land.

In the first place, this occurs every time rent proper is wiped out by the competition of new and more fertile soils; secondly, the improvements which might have been valuable at one time cease to be of value the moment they become universal owing to the development of agronomy.

The representative of land as capital is not the landlord, but the farmer. The proceeds yielded by land as capital are interest and industrial profit, not rent. There are lands which yield such interest and profit but still yield no rent.

Briefly, land in so far as it yields interest, is land capital, and as land capital it yields no rent, it is not landed property. Rent results from the social relations in which the exploitation of the land takes place. It cannot be a result of the more or less solid, more or less durable nature of the soil. Rent is a product of society and not of the soil.

According to M. Proudhon, "improvement in the use of the land"—a consequence "of the perfecting of industry"—causes the continual rise in rent. On the contrary, this improvement causes its periodical fall.

Wherein consists, in general, any improvement, whether in agriculture or in manufacture? In producing more with the same labour; in producing as much, or even more, with less labour. Thanks to these improvements, the farmer is spared from using a greater amount of labour for a relatively smaller product. He has no need, therefore, to resort to inferior soils, and instalments of capital applied successively to the same soil remain equally productive.

Thus, these improvements, far from continually raising rent as M. Proudhon says, become on the contrary so many temporary obstacles preventing its rise.

The English landowners of the seventeenth century were so well aware of this truth, that they opposed the progress of agriculture for fear of seeing their incomes diminish. (See Petty, an English economist of the time of Charles II.[44])

§5. STRIKES AND COMBINATIONS OF WORKERS

Every upward movement in wages can have no other effect than a rise in the price of corn, wine, etc., that is, the effect of a dearth. For what are wages? They are the cost price of corn, etc.; they are the integrant price of everything. We may go even further: wages are the proportion of the elements composing wealth and consumed reproductively every day by the mass of the workers. Now, to double wages ... is to attribute to each one of the producers a greater share than his product, which is contradictory, and if the rise extends only to a small number of industries, it brings about a general disturbance in exchange; in a word, a *dearth*.... It is impossible, I declare, for strikes followed by an increase in wages not to culminate in a *general rise in prices:* this is as certain as that two and two make four. (Proudhon, Vol. I, pp. 110 and 111.)

We deny all these assertions, except that two and two make four.

In the first place, there is no *general rise in prices*. If the price of everything doubles at the same time as wages, there is no change in price, the only change is in terms.

Then again, a general rise in wages can never produce a more or less general rise in the price of goods. Actually, if every industry employed the same number of workers in relation to fixed capital or to the instruments used, a general rise in wages would produce a general fall in profits and the current price of goods would undergo no alteration.

But as the relation of manual labour to fixed capital is not the same in different industries, all the industries which employ a relatively greater mass of capital and fewer workers, will be forced sooner or later to lower the price of their goods. In the opposite case, in which the price of their goods is not lowered, their profit will rise above the common rate of profits. Machines are not wage-earners. Therefore, the general rise in wages will affect less those industries, which, compared with the others, employ more machines than workers. But as competition always tends to level the rate of profits, those profits which rise above the average rate cannot but be transitory. Thus, apart from a few fluctuations, a general rise in wages will lead, not as M. Proudhon says, to a general increase in prices, but to a partial fall, that is a fall in the current price of the goods that are made chiefly with the help of machines.

The rise and fall of profits and wages expresses merely the proportion in which capitalists and workers share in the product of a day's work, without influencing in most instances the price of the product. But that "strikes followed by an increase in wages culminate in a general rise in prices, in a dearth even"—these are notions which can blossom only in the brain of a poet who has not been understood.

In England, strikes have regularly given rise to the invention and application of new machines. Machines were, it may be said, the weapon employed by the capitalists to quell the revolt of specialized labour. The *self-acting mule,* the greatest invention of modern industry, put out of action the spinners who were in revolt. If combinations and strikes had no other effect than that of making the efforts of mechanical genius react against them, they would still exercise an immense influence on the development of industry.

"I find," continues M. Proudhon,

in an article published by M. Léon Faucher ... September 1845,* that for some time the British workers have got out of the habit *of combination,* which is assuredly a progress for which one cannot but congratulate them: but this improvement in the morale of the workers comes chiefly from their economic education. "It is not on the manufacturers," cried a spinning-mill worker at a Bolton meeting, "that wages depend. In periods of depression

*L. Faucher, "Les coalitions condamnées par les ouvriers anglais."

the masters are, so to speak, merely the whip with which necessity arms itself, and whether they want to or not, they have to deal blows. The regulative principle is the relation of supply to demand; and the masters have not this power".... Well done! cries M. Proudhon, these are well-trained workers, model workers, etc., etc., etc. Such poverty did not exist in Britain; it will not cross the Channel. (Proudhon, Vol. I, pp. 261 and 262.)

Of all the towns in England, Bolton is the one in which radicalism is the most developed. The Bolton workers are known to be the most revolutionary of all. At the time of the great agitation in England for the abolition of the Corn Laws,[45] the English manufacturers thought that they could cope with the landowners only by thrusting the workers to the fore. But as the interests of the workers were no less opposed to those of the manufacturers than the interests of the manufacturers were to those of the landowners, it was natural that the manufacturers should fare badly in the workers' meetings. What did the manufacturers do? To save appearances they organized meetings composed, to a large extent, of foremen, of the small number of workers who were devoted to them, and of the real *friends of trade*. When later on the genuine workers tried, as in Bolton and Manchester, to take part in these sham demonstrations, in order to protest against them, they were forbidden admittance on the ground that it was a *ticket meeting*—a meeting to which only persons with entrance cards were admitted. Yet the posters placarded on the walls had announced public meetings. Every time one of these meetings was held, the manufacturers' newspapers gave a pompous and detailed account of the speeches made. It goes without saying that it was the foremen who made these speeches. The London papers reproduced them word for word. M. Proudhon has the misfortune to take foremen for ordinary workers, and enjoins them not to cross the Channel

If in 1844 and 1845 strikes drew less attention than before, it was because 1844 and 1845 were the first two years of prosperity that British industry had had since 1837.[46] Nevertheless none of the *trades unions* had been dissolved.

Now let us listen to the foremen of Bolton. According to them manufacturers have no command over wages because they have no command over the price of products, and they have no command over the price of products because they have no command over the world market. For this reason they wish it to be understood that combinations should not be formed to extort an increase in wages from the masters. M. Proudhon, on the contrary, forbids combinations for fear they should be followed by a rise in wages which would bring with it a general dearth. We have no need to say that on one point there is an *entente cordiale* between the foremen and M. Proudhon: that a rise in wages is equivalent to a rise in the price of products.

But is the fear of a dearth the true cause of M. Proudhon's rancour? No. Quite simply be is annoyed with the Bolton foremen because they determine value by *supply and demand* and hardly take any account of *constituted value,* of value which has passed into the state of constitution, of the constitution of value, including *permanent exchangeability* and all the other *proportionalities of relations and relations of proportionality,* with Providence at their side.

> A workers' strike is *illegal,* and it is not only the Penal Code that says so, it is the economic system, the necessity of the established order.... That each worker individually should dispose freely over his person and his hands, this can be tolerated, but that workers should undertake by combination to do violence to monopoly, is something society cannot permit. (Vol. I, pp. 334 and 335.)

M. Proudhon wants to pass off an article of the Penal Code as a necessary and general result of bourgeois relations of production.

In England combination is authorized by an Act of Parliament, and it is the economic system which has forced Parliament to grant this legal authorization. In 1825, when, under the Minister Huskisson, Parliament had to modify the law in order to bring it more and more into line with the conditions resulting from free competition, it had of necessity to abolish all laws forbidding combinations of workers.[47] The more modern industry and competition develop, the more elements there are which call forth and strengthen combination, and as soon as combination becomes an economic fact, daily gaining in solidity, it is bound before long to become a legal fact.

Thus the article of the Penal Code proves at the most that modern industry and competition were not yet well developed under the Constituent Assembly and under the Empire.[48]

Economists and Socialists* are in agreement on one point: the condemnation of *combinations.* Only they have different motives for their act of condemnation.

The economists say to the workers: Do not combine. By combination you hinder the regular progress of industry, you prevent manufacturers from carrying out their orders, you disturb trade and you precipitate the invasion of machines which, by rendering

---

* That is, the Socialists of that time: the Fourierists in France, the Owenites in England. *[Note by Engels to the German edition of 1885.]*

your labour in part useless, force you to accept a still lower wage.
Besides, whatever you do, your wages will always be determined
by the relation of hands demanded to hands supplied, and it is
an effort as ridiculous as it is dangerous for you to revolt against
the eternal laws of political economy.

The Socialists say to the workers: Do not combine, because
what will you gain by it anyway? A rise in wages? The economists will prove to you quite clearly that the few ha'pence you
may gain by it for a few moments if you succeed, will be followed
by a permanent fall. Skilled calculators will prove to you that it
would take you years merely to recover, through the increase in
your wages, the expenses incurred for the organization and upkeep of the combinations.

And we, as Socialists, tell you that, apart from the money
question, you will continue none the less to be workers, and the
masters will still continue to be the masters, just as before. So no
combination! No politics! For is not entering into combination
engaging in politics?

The economists want the workers to remain in society as it is
constituted and as it has been signed and sealed by them in
their manuals.

The Socialists want the workers to leave the old society alone,
the better to be able to enter the new society which they have
prepared for them with so much foresight.

In spite of both of them, in spite of manuals and utopias,
combination has not ceased for an instant to go forward and
grow with the development and growth of modern industry. It
has now reached such a stage, that the degree to which combination has developed in any country clearly marks the rank it
occupies in the hierarchy of the world market. England, whose
industry has attained the highest degree of development, has the
biggest and best organized combinations.

In England they have not stopped at partial combinations which
have no other objective than a passing strike, and which disappear
with it. Permanent combinations have been formed, *trades unions,*
which serve as ramparts for the workers in their struggles with the
employers. And at the present time all these local *trades unions*
find a rallying point in the *National Association of United Trades,*[49]
the central committee of which is in London, and which already
numbers 80,000 members. The organization of these strikes, combinations, and *trades unions* went on simultaneously with the political struggles of the workers, who now constitute a large political
party, under the name of Chartists.

The first attempts of workers to *associate* among themselves always take place in the form of combinations.

Large-scale industry concentrates in one place a crowd of people unknown to one another. Competition divides their interests. But the maintenance of wages, this common interest which they have against their boss, unites them in a common thought of resistance-*combination*. Thus combination always has a double aim, that of stopping competition among the workers, so that they can carry on general competition with the capitalist. If the first aim of resistance was merely the maintenance of wages, combinations, at first isolated, constitute themselves into groups as the capitalists in their turn unite for the purpose of repression, and in face of always united capital, the maintenance of the association becomes more necessary to them than that of wages. This is so true that English economists are amazed to see the workers sacrifice a good part of their wages in favour of associations, which, in the eyes of these economists, are established solely in favour of wages. In this struggle—a veritable civil war—all the elements necessary for a coming battle unite and develop. Once it has reached this point, association takes on a political character.

Economic conditions had first transformed the mass of the people of the country into workers. The combination of capital has created for this mass a common situation, common interests. This mass is thus already a class as against capital, but not yet for itself. In the struggle, of which we have noted only a few phases, this mass becomes united, and constitutes itself as a class for itself. The interests it defends become class interests. But the struggle of class against class is a political struggle.

In the bourgeoisie we have two phases to distinguish: that in which it constituted itself as a class under the regime of feudalism and absolute monarchy, and that in which, already constituted as a class, it overthrew feudalism and monarchy to make society into a bourgeois society. The first of these phases was the longer and necessitated the greater efforts. This too began by partial combinations against the feudal lords.

Much research has been carried out to trace the different historical phases that the bourgeoisie has passed through, from the commune up to its constitution as a class.

But when it is a question of making a precise study of strikes, combinations and other forms in which the proletarians carry out before our eyes their organization as a class, some are seized with real fear and others display a *transcendental* disdain.

An oppressed class is the vital condition for every society founded on the antagonism of classes. The emancipation of the oppressed class thus implies necessarily the creation of a new society. For the oppressed class to be able to emancipate itself it is necessary that the productive powers already acquired and the existing social relations should no longer be capable of existing side by side. Of all the instruments of production, the greatest productive power[50] is the revolutionary class itself. The organization of revolutionary elements as a class supposes the existence of all the productive forces which could be engendered in the bosom of the old society.

Does this mean that after the fall of the old society there will be a new class domination culminating in a new political power? No.

The condition for the emancipation of the working class is the abolition of every class, just as the condition for the liberation of the third estate, of the bourgeois order, was the abolition of all estates* and all orders.

The working class, in the course of its development, will substitute for the old civil society an association which will exclude classes and their antagonism, and there will be no more political power properly so-called, since political power is precisely the official expression of antagonism in civil society.

Meanwhile the antagonism between the proletariat and the bourgeoisie is a struggle of class against class, a struggle which carried to its highest expression is a total revolution. Indeed, is it at all surprising that a society founded on the opposition of classes should culminate in brutal *contradiction*, the shock of body against body, as its final *dénouement?*

Do not say that social movement excludes political movement. There is never a political movement which is not at the same time social.

It is only in an order of things in which there are no more classes and class antagonisms that *social evolutions* will cease to be *political revolutions*. Till then, on the eve of every general reshuffling of society, the last word of social science will always be:

"Le combat ou la mort; la lutte sanguinaire ou le néant. C'est ainsi que la question est invinciblement posse."

George Sand.[52]

---

* Estates here in the historical sense of the estates of feudalism, estates with definite and limited privileges. The revolution of the bourgeoisie abolished the estates and their privileges. Bourgeois society knows only *classes*. It was, therefore, absolutely in contradiction with history to describe the proletariat as the "fourth estate."[51] *[Note by F. Engels to the German edition, 1885.]*

APPENDICES

MARX TO P. V. ANNENKOV
Brussels, December 28, 1846

Dear Mr. Annenkov,

You would long ago have received my answer to your letter of November 1 but for the fact that my bookseller sent me Monsieur Proudhon's book, *The Philosophy of Poverty*, only last week. I have skimmed it in two days in order to be able to give you my opinion about it at once. As I have read the book very hurriedly, I cannot go into details but can only tell you the general impression it has made on me. If you wish I could go into details in a second letter.

I must frankly confess that I find the book on the whole poor, and very poor. You yourself laugh in your letter at the "patch of German philosophy" which M. Proudhon parades in this formless and pretentious work, but you suppose that the economic argument has not been infected by the philosophic poison. I too am very far from imputing the faults in the economic argument to M. Proudhon's philosophy. M. Proudhon does not give us a false criticism of political economy because he is the possessor of an absurd philosophic theory, but he gives us an absurd philosophic theory because he fails to understand the social system of today in its *engrènement* (intermeshing), to use a word which like much else M. Proudhon has borrowed from Fourier.

Why does M. Proudhon talk of God, of universal reason, of the impersonal reason of humanity which never errs, which has always been equal to itself throughout all the ages and of which one need only have the right consciousness in order to know the truth? Why does he resort to feeble Hegelianism to give himself the appearance of a bold thinker?

He himself provides you with the clue to this enigma. M. Proudhon sees in history a series of social developments; he finds progress realized in history; finally he finds that men, as individuals, did not know what they were doing and were mistaken about their own movement, that is to say, their social development seems at the first glance to be distinct, separate and independent of their individual development. He cannot explain these facts, and so he merely invents the hypothesis of the universal reason revealing itself. Nothing is easier than to invent mystical causes, that is to say, phrases which lack common sense.

But when M. Proudhon admits that he understands nothing about the historical development of humanity—he admits this by using such high-sounding words as: universal reason, God, etc.—is he not implicitly and necessarily admitting that he is incapable of understanding *economic development?*

What is society, whatever its form may be? The product of men's reciprocal action. Are men free to choose this or that form of society for themselves? By no means. Assume a particular state of development in the productive forces of man and you will get a particular form of commerce and consumption. Assume particular stages of development in production, commerce and consumption and you will have a corresponding social constitution, a corresponding organization of the family, of orders or of classes, in a word, a corresponding civil society. Assume a particular civil society and you will get particular political conditions which are only the official expression of civil society. M. Proudhon will never understand this because he thinks he is doing something great by appealing from the state to society—that is to say, from the official résumé of society to official society.

It is superfluous to add that men are not free to choose their *productive* forces—which are the basis of all their history—for every productive force is an acquired force, the product of former activity. The productive forces are therefore the result of practical human energy; but this energy is itself conditioned by the circumstances in which men find themselves, by the productive forces already acquired, by the social form which exists before they do, which they do not create, which is the product of the preceding generation. Because of this simple fact that every succeeding generation finds itself in possession of the productive forces acquired by the previous generation, which serve it as the raw material for new production, a coherence arises in human history, a history of humanity takes shape which is all the more a history of humanity as the productive forces of man and therefore his social relations have been more developed. Hence it necessarily follows that the social history of men is never anything but the history of their individual development, whether they are conscious of it or not. Their material relations are the basis of all their relations. These material relations are only the necessary forms in which their material and individual activity is realized.

M. Proudhon mixes up ideas and things. Men never relinquish what they have won, but this does not mean that they never relinquish the social form in which they have acquired certain productive forces. On the contrary, in order that they may not be deprived of the result attained, and forfeit the fruits of civilization, they are obliged, from the moment when the form of their commerce no longer corresponds to the productive forces acquired, to change all their traditional social forms. I am using the word "commerce" here in its widest sense, as we use *Verkehr* in German. For example: the privileges, the institution of guilds and corporations, the regulatory regime of the Middle Ages, were social relations that alone corresponded to the acquired productive forces and to the social condition which had previously existed and from which these institutions had arisen. Under the protection of the regime of corporations and regulations, capital was accumulated, overseas trade was developed, colonies were founded. But the fruits of this men would have forfeited if they bad tried to retain the forms under whose shelter these fruits had ripened. Hence burst two thunderclaps—the Revolutions of 1640 and 1688. All the old economic forms, the social relations corresponding to them, the political conditions which were the official expression of the old civil society, were destroyed in England. Thus the economic forms in which men produce, consume, and exchange, are *transitory and historical.* With the acquisition of new productive faculties, men change their mode of production and with the mode of production all the economic relations which are merely the necessary relations of this particular mode of production.

This is what M. Proudhon has not understood and still less demonstrated. M. Proudhon, incapable of following the real movement of history, produces a phantasmagoria which presumptuously claims to be dialectical. He does not feel it necessary to speak of the seventeenth, the eighteenth or the nineteenth century for his history proceeds in the misty realm of imagination and rises far above space and time. In short, it is not history but old Hegelian junk, it is not profane history—a history of man-but sacred history—a history of ideas. From his point of view man is only the instrument of which the idea or the eternal reason makes use in order to unfold itself. The *evolutions of* which M. Proudhon speaks are understood to be evolutions such as are accomplished within the mystic womb of the absolute idea. If you tear the veil from this mystical language, what it comes to is that M. Proudhon is offering you the order in which economic categories arrange themselves inside his own head. It will not require great exertion on my part to prove to you that it is the order of a very disorderly mind.

M. Proudhon begins his book with a dissertation on *value,* which is his pet subject. I will not enter on an examination of this dissertation today.

The series of economic evolutions of the eternal reason begins with *division of labour.* To M. Proudhon division of labour is a perfectly simple thing. But was not the caste regime also a particular division of labour? Was not the regime of the corporations another division of labour? And is not the division of labour under the system of manufacture, which in England begins about the middle of the seventeenth century and comes to an end in the last part of the eighteenth, also totally different from the division of labour in large-scale modern industry?

M. Proudhon is so far from the truth that he neglects what even the profane economists attend to. When he talks about division of labour he does not feel it necessary to mention the world *market.* Good. Yet must not the division of labour in the fourteenth and fifteenth centuries, when there were still no colonies, when America did not as yet exist for Europe, and Eastern Asia only existed for her through the medium of Constantinople, have been fundamentally different from what it was in the seventeenth century when colonies were already developed?

And that is not all. Is the whole inner organization of nations, are all their international relations anything else than the expression of a particular division of labour? And must not these change when the division of labour changes?

M. Proudhon has so little understood the problem of the division of labour that he never even mentions the separation of town and country, which took place in Germany, for instance, from the ninth to the twelfth century. Thus, to M. Proudhon, this separation is an eternal law since he knows neither its origin nor its development. All through his book he speaks as if this creation of a particular mode of production would endure until the end of time. All that M. Proudhon says about the division of labour is only a summary, and moreover a very superficial and incomplete summary, of what Adam Smith and a thousand others have said before him.

The second evolution is *machinery*. The connection between the division of labour and machinery is entirely mystical to M. Proudhon. Each kind of division of labour had its specific instruments of production. Between the middle of the seventeenth and the middle of the eighteenth century, for instance, people did not make everything by hand. There were machines, and very complicated ones, such as looms, ships, levers, etc.

Thus there is nothing more absurd than to see machinery as deriving from division of labour in general.

I may also remark, by the way, that just as M. Proudhon has not understood the origin of machinery, he has still less understood its development. One can say that up to the year 1825—the period of the first general crisis—the demands of consumption in general increased more rapidly than production, and the development of machinery was a necessary consequence of the needs of the market. Since 1825, the invention and application of machinery has been simply the result of the war between workers and employers. But this is only true of England. As for the European nations, they were driven to adopt machinery owing to English competition both in their home markets and on the world market. Finally, in North America the introduction of machinery was due both to competition with other countries and to lack of hands, that is, to the disproportion between the population of North America and its industrial needs. From these facts you can see what sagacity Monsieur Proudhon develops when he conjures up the spectre of competition as the third evolution, the antithesis to machinery!

Lastly and in general, it is altogether absurd to make *machinery* an economic category alongside with division of labour, competition, credit, etc.

Machinery is no more an economic category than the ox which draws the plough. The application of machinery in the present day is one of the relations of our present economic system, but the way in which machinery is utilized is totally distinct from the machinery itself. Powder remains the same whether it is used to wound a man or to dress his wounds.

M. Proudhon surpasses himself when he allows competition, monopoly, taxes or police, balance of trade, credit and property to develop inside his head in the order in which I have mentioned them. Nearly all credit institutions had been developed in England by the beginning of the eighteenth century, before the discovery of machinery. Public credit was only a fresh method of increasing taxation and satisfying the new demands created by the rise of the bourgeoisie to power. Finally the last category in M. Proudhon's system is constituted by *property*. In the real world, on the other hand, the division of labour and all M. Proudhon's other categories are social relations forming in their entirety what is today known as *property:* outside these relations bourgeois property is nothing but a metaphysical or juristic illusion. The property of a different epoch, feudal property, develops in a series of entirely different social relations. M. Proudhon, by establishing property as an independent relation, commits more than a mistake in method: he clearly shows that he has not grasped the bond which holds together all forms of *bourgeois* production, that he has not understood the *historical and transitory* character of the forms of production in a particular epoch. M. Proudhon, who does not regard our social institutions as historical products, who can understand neither their origin nor their development, can only produce dogmatic criticism of them.

M. Proudhon is therefore obliged to take refuge in a *fiction* in order to explain development. He imagines that division of labour, credit, machinery, etc., were all invented to serve his fixed idea, the idea of equality. His explanation is sublimely naive. These things were invented in the interests of equality but unfortunately they turned against equality. This constitutes his whole argument. In other words, he makes a gratuitous assumption and then, as the actual development contradicts his fiction at every step, he concludes that there is a contradiction. He conceals from you the fact that the contradiction exists solely between his fixed ideas and the real movement.

Thus, M. Proudhon, mainly because he lacks the historical knowledge, has not perceived that as men develop their productive forces, that is, as they live, they develop certain relations with one another and that the nature of these relations must necessarily change with the change and growth of the productive forces. He has not perceived that *economic categories* are only *abstract expressions* of these actual relations and only remain true while these relations exist. He therefore falls into the error of the bourgeois economists, who regard these economic categories as eternal and not as historical laws which are only laws for a particular historical development, for a definite development of the productive forces. Instead, therefore, of regarding the political-economic categories as abstract expressions of the real, transitory, historic social relations. Monsieur Proudhon, thanks to a mystic inversion, sees in the real relations only embodiments of these abstractions. These abstractions themselves are formulas which have been slumbering in the heart of God the Father since the beginning of the world.

But here our good M. Proudhon falls into severe intellectual convulsions. If all these economic categories are emanations from the heart of God, are the hidden and eternal life of man, how does it come about, first, that there is such a thing as development, and secondly, that M.

Proudhon is not a conservative? He explains these evident contradictions by a whole system of antagonisms.

To throw light on this system of antagonisms let us take an example.

Monopoly is a good thing, because it is an economic category and therefore an emanation of God. Competition is a good thing because it is also an economic category. But what is not good is the reality of monopoly and the reality of competition. What is still worse is the fact that competition and monopoly devour each other. What is to be done? As these two eternal ideas of God contradict each other, it seems obvious to him that there is also within the bosom of God a synthesis of them both, in which the evils of monopoly are balanced by competition and *vice versa*. As a result of the struggle between the two ideas only their good side will come into view. One must snatch this secret idea from God and then apply it and everything will be for the best; the synthetic formula which lies hidden in the darkness of the impersonal reason of man must be revealed. M. Proudhon does not hesitate for a moment to come forward as the revealer.

But look for a moment at real life. In the economic life of the present time you find not only competition and monopoly but also their synthesis, which is not a *formula* but a *movement*. Monopoly produces competition, competition produces monopoly. But this equation, far from removing the difficulties of the present situation, as the bourgeois economists imagine it does, results in a situation still more difficult and confused. If therefore you alter the basis on which present-day economic relations rest, if you destroy the *present mode* of production, then you will not only destroy competition, monopoly and their antagonism, but also their unity, their synthesis, the movement which is the real equilibrium of competition and monopoly.

Now I will give you an example of Monsieur Proudhon's dialectics.

Freedom and slavery constitute an antagonism. I need not speak of the good and bad sides of freedom nor, speaking of slavery, need I dwell on its bad sides. The only thing that has to be explained is its good side. We are not dealing with indirect slavery, the slavery of the proletariat, but with direct slavery, the slavery of the blacks in Surinam, in Brazil, in the Southern States of North America.

Direct slavery is as much the pivot of our industrialism today as machinery, credit, etc. Without slavery no cotton; without cotton no modern industry. Slavery has given value to the colonies; the colonies have created world trade; world trade is the necessary condition of large-scale machine industry. Thus, before the traffic in Negroes began, the colonies supplied the Old World with only very few products and made no visible change in the face of the earth. Slavery is therefore an economic category of the highest importance. Without slavery North America, the most progressive country, would be transformed into a patriarchal land. You have only to wipe North America off the map of the nations and you get anarchy, the total decay of trade and of modern civilization. But to do away with slavery is to wipe America off the map of the nations. And therefore, because it is an economic category, we find slavery in every nation since the world began. Modern nations have merely known how to disguise slavery of their own countries while they openly imported it into the New World. After these observations on slavery, how will our worthy M. Proudhon proceed? He will look for the synthesis between freedom and slavery, the golden mean or equilibrium between slavery and freedom.

Monsieur Proudhon has very well grasped the fact that men produce cloth, linen, silks, and it is a great merit on his part to have grasped this small amount! What he has not grasped is that these men, according to their abilities, also produce the *social relations amid* which they prepare cloth and linen. Still less has he understood that men, who produce their social relations in accordance with their material productivity, also produce *ideas, categories,* that is to say the abstract ideal expression of these same social relations. Thus the categories are no more eternal than the relations they express. They are historical and transitory products. For M. Proudhon, on the contrary, abstractions, categories are the primordial cause. According to him they, and not men, make history. The *abstraction,* the *category taken as such,* i.e., apart from men and their material activities, is of course immortal, unchangeable, unmoved; it is only one form of the being of pure reason; which is only another way of saying that the abstraction as such is abstract. An admirable tautology!

Thus, regarded as categories, economic relations for M. Proudhon are eternal formulas without origin or progress.

Let us put it in another way: M. Proudhon does not directly state that *bourgeois life* is for him an *eternal verity;* he states it indirectly by deifying the categories which express bourgeois relations in the form of thought,. He takes the products of bourgeois society for spontaneously arisen eternal beings, endowed with a life of their own, as soon as they present themselves to his mind in the form of categories, in the form of thought. So he does not rise above the bourgeois horizon. As he is operating with bourgeois ideas, the eternal truth of which he presupposes, he seeks a synthesis, an equilibrium of these ideas, and does not see that the present method by which they reach equilibrium is the only possible one.

Indeed he does what all good bourgeois do. They all tell you that in principle, that is, considered as abstract ideas, competition, monopoly, etc., are the only basis of life, but that in practice they leave much to be desired. They all want competition without the lethal effects of competition. They all want the impossible, namely, the conditions of bourgeois existence without the necessary consequences of those conditions. None of them understands that the bourgeois form of production is historical and transitory, just as the feudal form was. This mistake arises from the fact that the bourgeois man is to them the only possible basis of every society; they cannot imagine a society in which men have ceased to be bourgeois.

M. Proudhon is therefore necessarily *doctrinaire. To* him the historical movement which is turning the present-day world upside down reduces itself to the problem of discovering the correct equilibrium, the synthesis, of two bourgeois thoughts. And so the clever fellow is able by his cunning to discover the hidden thought of God, the unity of two isolated thoughts—which are only isolated because M. Proudhon has isolated them from practical life, from present-day production, that is, from the union of realities which they express.

In place of the great historical movement arising from the conflict between the productive forces already acquired by men and their social relations, which no longer correspond to these productive forces; in place of the terrible wars which are being prepared between the different classes within each nation and between different nations; in place of the practical and violent action of the masses by which alone these conflicts can be resolved—in place of this vast, prolonged and complicated movement, Monsieur Proudhon supplies the whimsical motion of his own head. So it is the men of learning that make history, the men who know how to purloin God's secret thoughts. The common people have only to apply their revelations. You will now understand why M. Proudhon is the declared enemy of every political movement. The solution of present problems does not lie for him in public action but in the dialectical rotations of his own mind. Since to him the categories are the motive force, it is not necessary to change practical life in order to change the categories. Quite the contrary. One must change the categories and the consequence will be a change in the existing society.

In his desire to reconcile the contradictions Monsieur Proudhon does not even ask if the very basis of those contradictions must not be overthrown. He is exactly like the political doctrinaire who wants to have the king and the chamber of deputies and the chamber of peers as integral parts of social life, as eternal categories. All he is looking for is a new formula by which to establish an equilibrium between these powers whose equilibrium consists precisely in the actual movement in which one power is now the conqueror and now the slave of the other. Thus in the eighteenth century a number of mediocre minds were busy finding the true formula which would bring the social estates, nobility, king, parliament, etc., into equilibrium, and they woke up one morning to find that there was in fact no longer any king, parliament or nobility. The true equilibrium in this antagonism was the overthrow of all the social relations which served as a basis for these feudal existences and for the antagonisms of these feudal existences.

Because M. Proudhon places eternal ideas, the categories of pure reason, on the one side and human beings and their practical life, which according to him is the application of these categories, on the other, one finds with him from the beginning a *dualism* between life and ideas, between soul and body, a dualism which recurs in many forms. You can see now that this antagonism is nothing but the incapacity of M. Proudhon to understand the profane origin and the profane history of the categories which he deifies.

My letter is already too long for me to speak of the absurd case which M. Proudhon puts up against communism. For the moment you will grant me that a man who has not understood the present state of society may be expected to understand still less the movement which is tending to overthrow it, and the literary expressions of this revolutionary movement.

The *sole point* on which I am in complete agreement with Monsieur Proudhon is in his dislike for sentimental socialistic day dreams. I had already, before him, drawn much enmity upon myself by ridiculing this sentimental, utopian, mutton-headed socialism. But is not M. Proudhon strangely deluding himself when he sets up his petty-bourgeois sentimentality—I am referring to his declamations about home, conjugal love and all such banalities—in opposition to socialist sentimentality, which in Fourier, for example, goes much deeper than the pretentious platitudes of our worthy Proudhon? He himself is so thoroughly conscious of the emptiness of his arguments, of his utter incapacity to speak about these things, that he bursts into violent explosions of rage, vociferation and righteous wrath [irae hominis probi], foams at the mouth, curses, denounces, cries shame and murder, beats his breast and boasts before God and man that he is not defiled by the socialist infamies! He does not seriously criticize socialist sentimentalities, or what he regards as such. Like a holy *man*, a pope, he excommunicates poor sinners and sings the glories of the petty bourgeoisie and of the miserable patriarchal and amorous illusions of the domestic hearth. And this is no accident. From head to foot M. Proudhon is the philosopher and economist of the petty bourgeoisie. In an advanced society the *petty bourgeois* is necessarily from his very position a socialist on the one side and an economist on the other; that is to say, he is dazed by the magnificence of the big bourgeoisie and has sympathy for the sufferings of the people. He is at once both bourgeois and man of the people. Deep down in his heart he flatters himself that he is impartial and has found the right equilibrium, which claims to be something different from mediocrity. A petty bourgeois of this type glorifies *contradiction* because contradiction is the basis of his existence. He is himself nothing but social contradiction in action. He must justify in theory what he is in practice, and M. Proudhon has the merit of being the scientific interpreter of the French petty bourgeoisie—a genuine merit, because the petty bourgeoisie will form an integral part of all the impending social revolutions.

I wish I could send you my book on political economy* with this letter, but it has so far been impossible for me to get this work, and the criticism of the German philosophers and Socialists of which I spoke to you in Brussels, printed. You would never believe the difficulties which a publication of this kind comes up against in Germany, from the police on the one hand and from the booksellers, who are themselves the interested representatives of all the tendencies I *am* attacking, on the other. And as for our own Party, it is not merely that it is poor, but a large section of the German Communist Party is also angry with me for opposing their utopias and declamations....

* *The German Ideology.*

MARX TO J. B. SCHWEITZER

London, January 24, 1865

Dear Sir,

Yesterday I received a letter in which you demand from me a detailed judgment of *Proudhon*. Lack of time prevents me from fulfilling your desire. Added to which I have none of his works to hand. However, in order to assure you of my good will I am hastily jotting down a brief sketch. You can complete it, add to it or cut it—in short do anything you like with it.[53]

Proudhon's earliest efforts I no longer remember. His school work about the *Langue Universelle [Universal Language]* shows with what little ceremony he attacked problems for the solution of which he lacked the first elements of knowledge.

His first work, *Quest ce que la propriété? [What Is Property?]*, is undoubtedly his best. It is epoch-making, if not from the novelty of its content, at least by the new and audacious way of coming out with everything. Of course "property" had been not only criticized in various ways but also *"done away with"* in the utopian manner by the French Socialists and Communists whose works he knew. In this book Proudhon's relation to Saint-Simon and Fourier is about the same as that of Feuerbach to Hegel. Compared with Hegel, Feuerbach is extremely poor. All the same he was epoch-making *after* Hegel because he laid *stress on* certain points which were disagreeable to the Christian consciousness but important for the progress of criticism, and which Hegel had left in mystic semi-obscurity.

Proudhon's still strong muscular style, if I may be allowed the expression, prevails in this book. And its style is in my opinion its chief merit.

Even where he is only reproducing old stuff, one can see that Proudhon has found it out for himself, that what he is saying is new to him and ranks as new. The provocative defiance laying hands on the economic "holy of holies," the brilliant paradox which made a mock of the ordinary bourgeois mind, the withering criticism, the bitter irony, and, revealed here and there behind these, a deep and genuine feeling of indignation at the infamy of the existing order, a revolutionary earnestness—all these electrified the readers of *What Is Property?* and produced a great sensation on its first appearance. In a strictly scientific history of political economy the book would hardly be worth mentioning. But sensational works of this kind play their part in the sciences just as much as in the history of the novel. Take, for instance, Malthus's book on *Population*. In its first edition it was nothing but a "sensational pamphlet" and *plagiarism* from beginning to end into the bargain. And yet what a *stimulus* was produced by this *libel on the human race!*

If I had Proudhon's book before me I could easily give a few examples to illustrate his early style. In the passages which he himself regarded as the most important he imitates Kant's treatment of the *antinomies*—Kant, whose works he had read in translations, was at that time the only German philosopher he knew—and he leaves one with a strong impression that to him, as to Kant, the resolution of the antinomies is something *"beyond"* the human understanding, i.e., something about which his own understanding is in the dark.

But in spite of all his apparent iconoclasm one already finds in *What Is Property?* the contradiction that Proudhon is criticizing society, on the one hand, from the standpoint and with the eyes of a French small peasant (later petty bourgeois) and, on the other, with the standards derived from his inheritance from the Socialists.

The deficiency of the book is indicated by its very title. The question was so falsely formulated that it could not be answered correctly. *Ancient "property relations"* were swallowed up by *feudal* property relations and these by *"bourgeois"* property relations. Thus history itself had practised its criticism upon past *property relations*. What Proudhon was actually dealing with was *modern bourgeois property* as it exists today. The question of what this is could only have been answered by a critical analysis of *"political economy,"* embracing these property *relations* as a whole, not in their legal expression as *voluntary retations* but in their real form, that is, as *relations of production*. But as he entangled the whole of these economic relations in the general juristic conception of *"property,"* Proudhon could not get beyond the answer which *Brissot,* in a similar work, had already, before 1789, given in the same words: *"*Property is theft.*"*

The most that can be got out of this is that the bourgeois juristic conceptions of *"theft"* apply equally well to the *"honest"* gains of the bourgeois himself. On the other hand, since theft as a forcible violation of property *presupposes the existence of property,* Proudhon entangled himself in all sorts of fantasies, obscure even to himself, about *true bourgeois property.*

During my stay in Paris in 1844 1 came into personal contact with Proudhon. I mention this here because to a certain extent I am also to blame for his *"sophistication,"* as the English call the adulteration of commercial goods. In the course of lengthy debates often lasting all night, I infected him to his great injury with Hegelianism, which, owing to his lack of German, he could not study properly. After my expulsion from Paris Herr *Karl Grün* continued what I had begun. As a teacher of German philosophy he also had the advantage over me that he understood nothing about it himself.

Shortly before the appearance of Proudhon's second important work, *Philosophie de la Misère, etc.,* he announced this to me himself in a very detailed letter in which he said, among other things: "I await the lash of your criticism." This soon fell upon him in my *Misère de la Philosophic, etc.,* Paris 1847, in a fashion which ended our friendship forever.

From what I have already said you can see that Proudhon's *Philoso-phie de la Misère ou Système des Contradictions économiques* first actu-ally contained his answer to the question *What Is Property?* In fact it was only after the publication of this latter work that be had begun his economic studies; he had discovered that the question be had raised could not be answered by *invective,* but only by an *analysis* of modern "political economy." At the same time he attempted to present the *sys-tem* of economic categories dialectically. In place of Kant's insoluble *"antinomies,"* the Hegelian *"contradiction"* was to be introduced as the means of development.

For an estimate of his book, which is in two fat volumes, I must refer you to the work I wrote as a reply.

There I showed, among other things, how little he has penetrated into the secret of scientific dialectics and how, on the contrary, he shares the illusions of speculative philosophy in his treatment of the *economic categories;* how instead of conceiving them as *the theoretical expression of historical relations of production, corresponding to a particular stage of development in material production,* be transforms them by his twad-dle into preexisting *eternal ideas,* and in this roundabout way arrives once more at the standpoint of bourgeois economy.*

I also show further how very deficient and sometimes even schoolboy-ish his knowledge is of the "political economy" which he undertook to criticize, and how he and the utopians are hunting for a so-called *"sci-ence"* by which a formula for the "solution of the social question" is to be excogitated a *priori,* instead of deriving their science from a critical knowledge of the historical movement, a movement which itself pro-duces the *material conditions of emancipation.* But especially I show how confused, wrong and superficial Proudhon remains with regard to *exchange value,* the basis of the whole thing, and how he even tries to use the utopian interpretation of *Ricardo's* theory of value as the basis of a new science. With regard to his general point of view I made the following comprehensive judgment:

> Every economic relation has a good and a bad side; it is the one point on which M. Proudhon does not give himself the lie. He sees the good side expounded by the economists; the bad side he sees denounced by the Socialists. He borrows from the economists the necessity of eternal relations; he borrows from the Socialists the illusion of seeing in poverty nothing but poverty (instead of seeing in it the revolutionary, subversive aspect which will overthrow the old society). He is in agreement with both in wanting to fall back upon the authority of science. Science for him reduces itself to the slender proportions of a scientific formula; he is the man in search of formulas. Thus it is that M. Proudhon flatters himself on having given a criticism of both political economy and communism: he is beneath them both. Beneath the economists, since, as a

---

* "When the economists say that present-day relations—the relations of bourgeois produc-tion—are natural, they imply that these are the relations in which wealth is created and productive forces developed in conformity with the laws of nature. These relations therefore are themselves *natural laws* independent of the influence of time. They are *eternal laws* which must always govern society. Thus there has been history, but there is no longer any" (p. 113 of my work). [Note by Marx.] [See present edition, pp. 88-89.—*Ed.*]

philosopher who has at his elbow a magic formula, he thought he could dispense with going into purely economic details; beneath the Socialists, because he has neither courage enough nor insight enough to rise, be it even speculatively, above the bourgeois horizon....

He wants to soar as the man of science above the bourgeois and the proletarians; *he is merely the petty bourgeois*, continually tossed back and forth between capital and labour, political economy and communism.54

Severe though the above judgment sounds I must still endorse every word of it today. At the same time, however, it must be remembered that at the time when I declared his book to be the petty-bourgeois code of socialism and proved this theoretically, Proudhon was still being branded as an extreme arch-revolutionary alike by the political economists and by the Socialists. That is why even later on I never joined in the outcry about his *"treachery"* to the revolution. It was not his fault that, originally misunderstood by other's as well as by himself, he failed to fulfil unjustified hopes.

In the *Philosophy of Poverty* all the defects of Proudhon's method of presentation stand out very unfavourably in comparison with *What Is Property?* The style is often what the French call *ampoulé* [*bombastic*]. Highsounding speculative jargon, supposed to be German-philosophical, appears regularly on the scene when his Gallic acuteness of understanding fails him. A self-advertising, self-glorifying, boastful tone and especially the twaddle about *"science"* and sham display of it, which are always so unedifying, are continually screaming in one's ears. Instead of the genuine warmth which glowed in his first attempt, here certain passages are systematically worked up into a momentary beat by rhetoric. Add to this the clumsy distasteful erudition of the self-taught, whose primitive pride in his own original thought has already been broken and who now as *a parvenu* of science, feels it necessary to bolster himself up with what he is not and has not. Then the mentality of the petty bourgeois who in an indecently brutal way—and neither acutely nor profoundly nor even correctly—attacks a man like *Cabet*, to be respected for his practical attitude towards the proletariat, while he flatters a man like *Dunoyer* (a "State Councillor," it is true). Yet the whole significance of this Dunoyer lay in the comic zeal with which, throughout three fat, unbearably boring volumes, he preached the rigourism characterized by Helvetius as *"On veut que les malheureux soient parfaits"* (demanding that the unfortunate should be perfect).

The February Revolution certainly came at a very inconvenient moment for Proudhon, who had irrefutably proved only a few weeks before that "the *era of revolutions*" was past for ever. His coming forward in the National Assembly, however little insight it showed into existing conditions, was worthy of every praise. After the June insurrection it was an act of great courage. In addition it had the fortunate consequence that M. Thiers, by his speech opposing Proudhon's proposals, which was then issued as a special publication, proved to the whole of Europe on what a pedestal of children's catechism the intellectual pillar of the French bourgeoisie was based. Indeed, compared with M. *Thiers, Proudhon* expanded to the size of an antediluvian colossus.

Proudhon's discovery of *"Crédit gratuit"* [free credit] and the *"banque du peuple"* [people's bank] based upon it, were his last economic "deeds." In my book *A Contribution to the Critique of Political Economy,* Part I, Berlin 1859 (pp. 59-64), will be found the proof that the theoretical basis of his idea arises from a misunderstanding of the first elements of bourgeois "political economy," namely of the relation between *commodities* and money" while the practical superstructure is simply a reproduction of much older and far better developed schemes.

That under certain economic and political conditions the credit system can serve to hasten the emancipation of the working class, just as, for instance, in the beginning of the eighteenth and again at the beginning of the nineteenth century in England, it served towards transferring the wealth of one class to another, is quite unquestionable, self-evident. But to regard *interest-bearing capital as the main form of capital* while trying to use a special form of credit, the alleged abolition of interest, as the basis for a transformation of society is a *thoroughly petty-bourgeois* fantasy. Hence indeed this fantasia, eked out further, is already to be found among *the economic spokesmen of the English petty bourgeoisie in the seventeenth century.* Proudhon's polemic with Bastiat (1850) about interest-bearing capital is on a far lower level than the *Philosophy of Poverty.* He succeeds in getting himself beaten even by Bastiat and breaks into burlesque bluster when his opponent drives his blows home.

A few years ago Proudhon—instigated I think by the government of Lausanne—wrote a prize essay on *Taxation.* Here the last flicker of genius is extinguished. Nothing remains but the petty bourgeois pure and simple.

So far as his political and philosophical writings are concerned they all show the same contradictory, dual character as his economic works. Moreover, their value is confined to France alone. Nevertheless his attacks on religion, the church, etc., were of great merit in his own country at a time when the French Socialists thought it desirable to show by their religiosity how superior they were to the bourgeois Voltairianism of the eighteenth century and the German godlessness of the nineteenth. If Peter the Great defeated Russian barbarism by barbarity, Proudhon did his best to defeat French phrasemongering by phrases. His work on the *Coup d'état,* in which he flirts with Louis Bonaparte and, in fact, strives to make him palatable to the French workers, and his last work, written against *Poland,* in which for the greater glory of the tsar he expresses the cynicism of a cretin, must be characterized as not merely bad but base productions; of a baseness which corresponds, however, to the petty-bourgeois point of view.

Proudhon has often been compared to *Rousseau. Nothing* could be more erroneous. He is more like *Nicolas Linguet,* whose *Théorie des lois civiles,* by the way, is a very brilliant book.

Proudhon had a natural inclination for dialectics. But as he never grasped really scientific dialectics he never got further than sophistry. In fact this hung together with his petty-bourgeois point of view. Like the historian *Raumer*, the petty bourgeois is composed of On The One Hand and On The Other Hand. This is so in his economic interests and *therefore* in his politics, in his scientific, religious and artistic views. It is so in his morals, in everything. He is a living contradiction. If, like Proudhon, he is in addition a gifted man, he will soon learn to play with his own contradictions and develop them according to circumstances into striking, ostentatious, now scandalous or now brilliant paradoxes. Charlatanism in science and accommodation in politics are inseparable from such a point of view. There only remains one governing motive, the *vanity* of the subject, and the only question for him, as for all vain people, is the success of the moment, the attention of the day. Thus the simple moral sense, which always kept a Rousseau, for instance, far from even the semblance of compromise with the powers that be, is necessarily extinguished.

Perhaps future generations will sum up the latest phase of French development by saying that Louis Bonaparte was its Napoleon and Proudhon its Rousseau-Voltaire.

And now you must take upon yourself the responsibility of having imposed upon me the role of this man's judge so soon after his death.

Yours very respectfully,

Karl Marx

FROM MARX'S WORK:
A CONTRIBUTION TO THE CRITIQUE OF POLITICAL ECONOMY
Berlin, 1859, pp. 61-64

The theory of labour time as an immediate money unit was first systematically developed by John Gray.*

He causes a national Central Bank through its branches to certify the labour time expended in the production of the various commodities. In exchange for the commodity, the producer receives an official certificate of the value, i.e., a receipt for as much labour time as his commodity contains,** and these bank-notes of one labour

---

* John Gray: *The Social System, etc. A Treatise on the Principle of Exchange*, Edinburgh 1831. Compare *Lectures on the Nature and Use of Money*, Edinburgh 1848, by the same author. After the February Revolution, Gray sent a memorandum to the French Provisional Government, in which he argued that France was not in need of an "organization of labour," but of an "organization of exchange," the plan of which, fully worked out, was contained in the system of money which he had invented. The good John had no inkling that sixteen years after the appearance of *The Social System* a patent for the same discovery would be taken out by the inventive Proudhon.

** Gray, *The Social System, etc.*, p. 63. "Money should be merely a receipt, an evidence that the holder of it has either contributed a certain value to the national stock of wealth, or that he has acquired a right to the said value from some one who has contributed to it."

week, one labour day, one labour hour, etc., serve at the same time as a claim on the equivalent in allcommodities stored in the warehouses of the bank.* This is the basic principle carefully worked out in detil and throughout adapted to existing English institutions. With this system, says Gray, "to sell for money may be rendered, at all times, precisely as easy as it now is to buy with money; production would become the uniform and never failing cause of demand."** The precious metals would lose their "privilege" over other commodities and would "take their proper place in the market beside butter and eggs, and cloth and calico, and then the value of the precious metals will concern us just as little as the value of the diamond."*** "Shall we retain our fictitious standard of value, gold, and thus keep the productive resources of the country, in bondage? or, shall we resort to the natural standard of value, labour, and thereby set our productive resources free?"****

Since labour time is the immanent measure of value, why have another external measure alongside of it? Why does exchange value develop into price? Why do all commodities have their values estimated in one exclusive commodity, which is thus transformed into the adequate existence of exchange value, into money? This was the problem that Gray had to solve. Instead of solving it, he imagines that commodities can have an immediate relation to one another as products of social labour. They can, however, only have a relation to one another as what they are. Commodities are, immediately, products of isolated, independent, private pieces of labour which must be sanctioned as general social labour by their alienation in the process of private exchange, or labour on the basis of commodity production only becomes social labour by the all-round alienation of the individual pieces of work. But if Gray substitutes the labour time contained in the commodities as *immediately social*, then he substitutes it as social labour or the labour time of directly associated individuals. Thus, in fact, a specific commodity, like gold or silver, would not be able to be contrasted with other commodities as the incarnation of general labour, exchange value would not become price, neither would use value also become exchange value, the product would not become a commodity and so the basis of bourgeois production would be done away with. But this is by no means Gray's opinion. *Products are to be produced as commodities but not to be exchanged as commodities.*

Gray hands over to a national Bank the execution of this pious wish. On the one hand, society in the form of the bank makes the individuals dependent on the conditions of private exchange, and, on the other

---

* "An estimated value being previously put upon produce, let it be lodged in a bank, and drawn out again whenever it is required; merely stipulating, by common consent, that he who lodges any kind of property in the proposed national Bank, may take out of it an equal value of whatever it may contain, instead of being obliged to draw out the self-same thing that he put in." *Loc. cit.*, p. 68.

** *Loc. cit.*, p. 16.

*** Gray, *Lectures on Money, etc.*, pp. 182-183.

**** *Loc. cit.*, p. 169.

hand, society makes them continue to produce on the basis of private exchange. Inner logic meanwhile drives Gray to renounce one bourgeois condition of production after another, although he only wants to "reform" money arising out of commodity exchange. Thus, he converts capital into national capital,* landed property into national property,** and if his bank is examined closely it will be found that it does not merely receive commodities with one hand and with the other give out certificates of labour supplied, but that it regulates production itself. In his last work, *Lectures on Money*, in which Gray anxiously tries to represent his labour money as a purely bourgeois reform, he entangles himself in still more blatant nonsense.

Every commodity is immediately money. This was Gray's theory, derived from his incomplete and consequently false analysis of commodities. The "organic" construction of "labour money" and "national bank" and "commodity warehouses" is only a dream picture, in which dogma is palmed off as a universal law. The dogma that a commodity is immediately money, or that the particular labour of the private individual contained in it is immediately social labour, naturally does not become true by a bank believing in it and operating according to it. Bankruptcy would in such a case most likely take the place of practical criticism. What is concealed in Gray and indeed remains a secret even to himself, viz., that labour money is an economic-sounding phrase for the pious wish to get rid of money, and with money to get rid of exchange value, and with exchange value to get rid of commodities, and with commodities to get rid of the bourgeois system of production, this is spoken out point-blank by some English Socialists who have written partly before and partly after Gray.*** But it has been reserved for *Proudhon* and his school to preach seriously the degradation of *money* and the ascent to heaven of *commodities* as the kernel of socialism and thereby to resolve socialism into an elementary misunderstanding of the necessary connection between commodities and money.****

* "The business of every nation will be conducted upon the basis of a national capital." (John Gray: *The Social System, etc.*, p. 171.)

** "The land to be converted into national property." (*Loc. cit.*, p. 298.)

*** See e.g., W. Thompson: *An Inquiry into the Distribution of Wealth, etc.* London 1824; Bray: *Labour's Wrongs and Labour's Remedy.* Leeds 1839.

**** As a compendium of this melodramatic theory of money can be regarded: Alfred Darimont: *De la réforme des banques*, Paris 1856.

ON THE QUESTION OF FREE TRADE

Public Speech Delivered by Karl Marx before the Democratic Association of Brussels, January 9, 1848[55]

Gentlemen,

The Repeal of the Corn Laws in England is the greatest triumph of free trade in the nineteenth century. In every country where manufacturers talk of free trade, they have in mind chiefly free trade in corn and raw materials in general. To impose protective duties on foreign corn is infamous, it is to speculate on the famine of peoples.

Cheap food, high wages, this is the sole aim for which English free-traders have spent millions, and their enthusiasm has already spread to their brethren on the Continent. Generally speaking, those who wish for free trade desire it in order to alleviate the condition of the working class.

But, strange to say, the people for whom cheap food is to be procured at all costs are very ungrateful. Cheap food is as ill-esteemed in England as cheap government is in France. The people see in these self-sacrificing gentlemen, in Bowring, Bright and Co., their worst enemies and the most shameless hypocrites.

Every one knows that in England the struggle between Liberals and Democrats takes the name of the struggle between Free Traders and Chartists.

Let us see now how the English free-traders have proved to the people the good intentions that animate them.

This is what they said to the factory workers:

"The duty levied on corn is a tax upon wages; this tax you pay to the landlords, those mediæval aristocrats; if your position is a wretched one, it is on account of the dearness of the immediate necessities of life."

The workers in turn asked the manufacturers:

"How is it that in the course of the last thirty years, while our industry has undergone the greatest development, our wages have fallen far more rapidly, in proportion, than the price of corn has gone up?

"The tax which you say we pay the landlords is about three pence a week per worker. And yet the wages of the hand-loom weaver fell, between 1815 and 1843, from 28s. per week to 5s., and the wages of the power-loom weavers, between 1823 and 1843, from 20s. per week to 8s.

"And during the whole of this period that portion of the tax which we paid to the landlord has never exceeded three pence. And, then, in the year 1834, when bread was very cheap and business going on very well, what did you tell us? You said, 'If you are unfortunate, it is because you have too many children, and your marriages are more productive than your labour!'

"These are the very words you spoke to us, and you set about making new Poor Laws, and building workhouses, those Bastilles of the proletariat."

To this the manufacturers replied:

"You are right, worthy labourers; it is not the price of corn alone, but competition of the hands among themselves as well, which determines wages.

"But ponder well one thing, namely, that our soil consists only of rocks and sandbanks. You surely do not imagine that corn can be grown in flower-pots. So if, instead of lavishing our capital and our labour upon a thoroughly sterile soil, we were to give up agriculture, and devote ourselves exclusively to industry, all Europe would abandon its factories, and England would form one huge factory town, with the whole of the rest of Europe for its countryside."

While thus haranguing his own workingmen, the manufacturer is interrogated by the small trader, who says to him:

"If we repeal the Corn Laws, we shall indeed ruin agriculture; but for all that, we shall not compel other nations to give up their own factories and buy from ours.

"What will the consequence be? I shall lose the customers that I have at present in the country, and the home trade will lose its market."

The manufacturer, turning his back upon the workers, replies to the shopkeeper:

"As to that, you leave it to us! Once rid of the duty on corn, we shall import cheaper corn from abroad. Then we shall reduce wages at the very time when they rise in the countries where we get our corn.

"Thus in addition to the advantages which we already enjoy we shall also have that of lower wages and, with all these advantages, we shall easily force the Continent to buy from us."

But now the farmers and agricultural labourers join in the discussion.

"And what, pray, is to become of us?

"Are we going to pass a sentence of death upon agriculture, from which we get our living? Are we to allow the soil to be torn from beneath our feet?"

As its whole answer the Anti-Corn Law League has contented itself with offering prizes for the three best essays upon the wholesome influence of the repeal of the Corn Laws on English agriculture.

These prizes were carried off by Messrs. Hope, Morse and Greg, whose essays were distributed in thousands of copies throughout the countryside.

The first of the prize-winners devotes himself to proving that neither the tenant farmer nor the agricultural labourer will lose by the free importation of foreign corn, but only the landlord. "The English tenant farmer," he exclaims,

> need not fear the repeal of the Corn Laws, because no other country can produce such good corn so cheaply as England.
>
> Thus, even if the price of corn fell, it would not hurt you, because this fall would only affect rent, which would go down, and not at all industrial profit and wages, which would remain stationary.

The second prize-winner, Mr. Morse, maintains, on the contrary, that the price of corn will rise in consequence of repeal. He takes infinite pains to prove that protective duties have never been able to secure a remunerative price for corn.

In support of his assertion he cites the fact that, whenever foreign corn has been imported, the price of corn in England has gone up considerably, and that when little corn has been imported, the price has fallen extremely. This prize-winner forgets that the importation was not the cause of the high price, but that the high price was the cause of the importation.

And in direct contradiction to his co-prize-winner, he asserts that every rise in the price of corn is profitable to both the tenant farmer and the labourer, but not to the landlord.

The third prize-winner, Mr. Greg, who is a big manufacturer and whose work is addressed to the large tenant farmers, could not hold with such stupidities. His language is more scientific.

He admits that the Corn Laws can raise rent only by raising the price of corn, and that they can raise the price of corn only by compelling capital to apply itself to land of inferior quality, and this is explained quite simply.

In proportion as population increases, if foreign corn cannot be imported, less fertile soil has to be used, the cultivation of which involves more expense and the product of this soil is consequently dearer.

There being a forced sale for corn, the price will of necessity be determined by the price of the product of the most costly soil. The difference between this price and the cost of production upon soil of better quality constitutes the rent.

If, therefore, as a result of the repeal of the Corn Laws, the price of corn, and consequently the rent, falls, it is because inferior soil will no longer be cultivated. Thus, the reduction of rent must inevitably ruin a part of the tenant farmers.

These remarks were necessary in order to make Mr. Greg's language comprehensible. He says:

> The small farmers, who cannot support themselves by agriculture will find a resource in industry. As to the large tenant farmers, they cannot fail to profit. Either the landlords will be obliged to sell them land very cheap, or leases will be made out for very long periods. This will enable tenant farmers to apply large sums of capital to the land, to use agricultural machinery on a larger scale, and to save manual labour, which will, moreover, be cheaper, on account of the general fall in wages, the immediate consequence of the repeal of the Corn Laws.

Dr. Bowring conferred upon all these arguments the consecration of religion, by exclaiming at a public meeting, "Jesus Christ is Free Trade, and Free Trade is Jesus Christ."

One can understand that all this hypocrisy was not calculated to make cheap bread attractive to the workers.

Besides, how could the workingman understand the sudden philanthropy of the manufacturers, the very men still busy fighting against the Ten Hour's Bill, which was to reduce the working day of the mill hands from twelve hours to ten?

To give you an idea of the philanthropy of these manufacturers I would remind you, gentlemen, of the factory regulations in force in all the mills.

Every manufacturer has for his own private use a regular penal code in which fines are laid down for every voluntary or involuntary offence. For instance, the worker pays so much if he has the misfortune to sit down on a chair; if he whispers, or speaks, or laughs; if he arrives a few moments too late; if any part of the machine breaks, or he does not turn out work of the quality desired, etc., etc. The fines are always greater than the damage really done by the worker. And to give the worker every opportunity for incurring fines, the factory clock is set forward, and he is given bad raw material to make into good pieces of stuff. An overseer not sufficiently skillful in multiplying cases of infraction of rules is discharged.

You see, gentlemen, this private legislation is enacted for the especial purpose of creating such infractions, and infractions are manufactured for the purpose of making money. Thus the manufacturer uses every means of reducing the nominal wage, and of profiting even by accidents over which the worker has no control.

These manufacturers are the same philanthropists who have tried to make the workers believe that they were capable of going to immense expense for the sole purpose of ameliorating their lot. Thus, on the one hand, they nibble at the wages of the worker in the pettiest way, by means of factory regulations, and, on the other, they are undertaking the greatest sacrifices to raise those wages again by means of the Anti-Corn Law League.

They build great palaces at immense expense, in which the League takes up, in some respects, its official residence; they send an army of missionaries to all corners of England to preach the gospel of free trade; they have printed and distributed gratis thousands of pamphlets to enlighten the worker upon his own interests, they spend enormous sums to make the press favourable to their cause; they organize a vast administrative system for the conduct of the free trade movement, and they display all their wealth of eloquence at public meetings. It was at one of these meetings that a worker cried out:

> If the landlords were to sell our bones, you manufacturers would be the first to buy them in order to put them through a steam-mill and make flour of them.

The English workers have very well understood the significance of the struggle between the landlords and the industrial capitalists. They know very well that the price of bread was to be reduced in order to reduce wages, and that industrial profit would rise by as much as rent fell.

Ricardo, the apostle of the English free-traders, the most eminent economist of our century, entirely agrees with the workers upon this point. In his celebrated work on political economy, he says:

> If instead of growing our own corn ... we discover a new market from which we can supply ourselves ... at a cheaper price, wages will fall and profits rise. The

fall in the price of agricultural produce reduces the wages, not only of the labourer employed in cultivating the soil, but also of all those employed in commerce or manufacture.[56]

And do not believe, gentlemen, that it is a matter of indifference to the worker whether he receives only four francs on account of corn being cheaper, when he had been receiving five francs before.

Have not his wages always fallen in comparison with profit, and is it not clear that his social position has grown worse as compared with that of the capitalist? Besides which he loses more as a matter of fact.

So long as the price of corn was higher and wages were also higher, a small saving in the consumption of bread sufficed to procure him other enjoyments. But as soon as bread is very cheap, and wages are therefore very cheap, he can save almost nothing on bread for the purchase of other articles.

The English workers have made the English free-traders realize that they are not the dupes of their illusions or of their lies; and if, in spite of this, the workers made common cause with them against the landlords, it was for the purpose of destroying the last remnants of feudalism and in order to have only one enemy left to deal with. The workers have not miscalculated, for the landlords, in order to revenge themselves upon the manufacturers, made common cause with the workers to carry the Ten Hours' Bill, which the latter had been vainly demanding for thirty years, and which was passed immediately after the repeal of the Corn Laws.

When Dr. Bowring, at the Congress of Economists,[57] drew from his pocket a long list to show how many head of cattle, how much ham, bacon, poultry, etc. , was imported into England, to be consumed, as he asserted, by the workers, he unfortunately forgot to tell you that at the time the workers of Manchester and other factory towns were finding themselves thrown on the streets by the crisis which was beginning.

As a matter of principle in political economy, the figures of a single year must never be taken as the basis for formulating general laws. One must always take the average period of from six to seven years—a period of time during which modern industry passes through the various phases of prosperity, overproduction, stagnation, crisis, and completes its inevitable cycle.

Doubtless, if the price of all commodities falls—and this is the necessary consequence of free trade—I can buy far more for a franc than before. And the worker's franc is as good as any other man's. Therefore, free trade will be very advantageous to the worker. There is only one little difficulty in this, namely, that the worker, before he exchanges his franc for other commodities, has first exchanged his labour with the capitalist. If in this exchange he always received the said franc for the same labour and the price of all other commodities fell, he would always be the gainer by such a bargain. The difficult point does not lie in proving that, if the price of all commodities falls, I will get more commodities for the same money.

Economists always take the price of labour at the moment of its exchange with other commodities. But they altogether ignore the moment at which labour accomplishes its own exchange with capital.

When less expense is required to set in motion the machine which produces commodities, the things necessary for the maintenance of this machine, called a worker, will also cost less. If all commodities are cheaper, labour, which is a commodity too, will also fall in price, and, as we shall see later, this commodity, labour, will fall far lower in proportion than the other commodities. If the worker still pins his faith to the arguments of the economists, he will find that the franc has melted away in his pocket, and that he has only five sous left.

Thereupon the economists will tell you:

> Well, we admit that competition among the workers, which will certainly not have diminished under free trade, will very soon bring wages into harmony with the low price of commodities. But, on the other hand, the low price of commodities will increase consumption, the larger consumption will require increased production, which will be followed by a larger demand for hands, and this larger demand for hands will be followed by a rise in wages.

The whole line of argument amounts to this: Free trade increases productive forces. If industry keeps growing, if wealth, if the productive power, if, in a word, productive capital increases, the demand for labour, the price of labour, and consequently the rate of wages, rise also.

The most favourable condition for the worker is the growth of capital. This must be admitted. If capital remains stationary, industry will not merely remain stationary but will decline, and in this case the worker will be the first victim. He goes to the wall before the capitalist. And in the case where capital keeps growing, in the circumstances which we have said are the best for the worker, what will be his lot? He will go to the wall just the same. The growth of productive capital implies the accumulation and the concentration of capital. The centralization of capital involves a greater division of labour and a greater use of machinery. The greater division of labour destroys the especial skill of the labourer; and by putting in the place of this skilled work labour which any one can perform, it increases competition among the workers.

This competition becomes fiercer as the division of labour enables a single worker to do the work of three. Machinery accomplishes the same result on a much larger scale. The growth of productive capital, which forces the industrial capitalists to work with constantly increasing means, ruins the small industrialists and throws them into the proletariat. Then, the rate of interest failing in proportion as capital accumulates, the small *rentiers*, who can no longer live on their dividends, are forced to go into industry and thus swell the number of proletarians.

Finally, the more productive capital increases, the more it is compelled to produce for a market whose requirements it does not know, the more production precedes consumption, the more supply tries to force demand, and consequently crises increase in frequency and in intensity. But every crisis in turn hastens the centralization of capital and adds to the proletariat.

Thus, as productive capital grows, competition among the workers grows in a far greater proportion. The reward of labour diminishes for all, and the burden of labour increases for some.

In 1829, there were in Manchester 1,088 cotton spinners employed in 36 factories. In 1841, there were no more than 448, and they tended 53,353 more spindles than the 1,088 spinners did in 1829. If manual labour had increased in the same proportion as the productive power, the number of spinners ought to have reached the figure of 1,848; improved machinery had, therefore, deprived 1,100 workers of employment.

We know beforehand the reply of the economists. The men thus deprived of work, they say, will find other kinds of employment. Dr. Bowring did not fail to reproduce this argument at the Congress of Economists, but neither did he fail to supply his own refutation.

In 1835, Dr. Bowring made a speech in the House of Commons upon the 50,000 hand-loom weavers of London who for a very long time had been starving without being able to find that new kind of employment which the free-traders hold out to them in the distance. We will give the most striking passages of this speech of Dr. Bowring:[58]

> This distress of the weavers ... is an inevitable condition of a species of labour easily learned—and constantly intruded on and superseded by cheaper means of production. A very short cessation of demand, where the competition for work is so great ... produces a crisis. The hand-loom weavers are on the verge of that state beyond which human existence can hardly be sustained, and a very trifling check hurls them into the regions of starvation.... The improvements of machinery, ... by superseding manual labour more and more, infallibly bring with them in the transition much of temporary suffering.... The national good cannot be purchased but at the expense of some individual evil. No advance was ever made in manufactures but at some cost to those who are in the rear; and of all discoveries, the power-loom is that which most directly bears on the condition of the hand-loom weaver. He is already beaten out of the field in many articles; he will infallibly be compelled to surrender many more.

Further on he says:

> I hold in my hand the correspondence which has taken place between the Governor-General of India and the East-India Company, on the subject of the Dacca hand-loom weavers.... Some years ago the East-India Company annually received of the produce of the looms of India to the amount of from 6,000,000 to 8,000,000 of pieces of cotton goods. The demand gradually fell to somewhat more than 1,000,000, and has now nearly ceased altogether. In 1800, the United States took from India nearly 800,000 pieces of cottons; in 1830, not 4,000. In 1800, 1,000,000 pieces were shipped to Portugal; in 1830, only 20,000. Terrible are the accounts of the wretchedness of the poor Indian weavers, reduced to absolute starvation. And what was the sole cause? The presence of the cheaper English manufacture.... Numbers of them 'died of hunger; the remainder were, for the most part, transferred to other occupations, principally agricultural. Not to have changed their trade was inevitable starvation. And at this moment that Dacca district is supplied with yarn and cotton cloth from the power-looms of England.... The Dacca muslins, celebrated over the whole world for their beauty and fineness, are also annihilated from the same cause. And

the present suffering, to numerous classes in India, is scarcely to be paralleled in the history of commerce.

Dr. Bowring's speech is the more remarkable because the facts quoted by him are exact, and the phrases with which he seeks to palliate them are wholly characterized by the hypocrisy common to all free trade sermons. He represents the workers as means of production which must be superseded by less expensive means of production. He pretends to see in the labour of which he speaks a wholly exceptional kind of labour, and in the machine which has crushed out the weavers an equally exceptional machine. He forgets that there is no kind of manual labour which may not any day be subjected to the fate of the hand-loom weavers.

It is, in fact, the constant aim and tendency of every improvement in machinery to supersede human labour altogether, or to diminish its cost by substituting the industry of women and children for that of men; or that of ordinary labourers for trained artisans. In most of the water-twist, or throstle cotton-mills, the spinning is entirely managed by females of sixteen years and upwards. The effect of substituting the self-acting mule for the common mule, is to discharge the greater part of the men spinners, and to retain adolescents and children.[59]

These words of the most enthusiastic free-trader, Dr. Ure, serve to complement the confessions of Dr. Bowring. Dr. Bowring speaks of certain individual evils, and, at the same time, says that these individual evils destroy whole classes; be speaks of the temporary sufferings during the transition period, and at the very time of speaking of them, he does not deny that these temporary evils have implied for the majority the transition from life to death, and for the rest a transition from a better to a worse condition. if he asserts, farther on, that the sufferings of these workers are inseparable from the progress of industry, and are necessary to the prosperity of the nation, he simply says that the prosperity of the bourgeois class presupposes as necessary the suffering of the labouring class.

All the consolation which Dr. Bowring offers the workers who perish, and, indeed, the whole doctrine of compensation which the free-traders propound, amounts to this:

You thousands of workers who are perishing, do not despair! You can die with an easy conscience. Your class will not perish. It will always be numerous enough for the capitalist class to decimate it without fear of annihilating it. Besides, how could capital be usefully applied if it did not take care always to keep up its exploitable material, i.e., the workers, to exploit them over and over again?

But, besides, why propound as a problem still to be solved the question: What influence will the adoption of free trade have upon the condition of the working class? All the laws formulated by the political economists from Quesnay to Ricardo have been based upon the hypothesis that the trammels which still interfere with commercial freedom have disappeared. These laws are confirmed in proportion as free trade is adopted. The first of these laws is that competition reduces the price of every commodity to the minimum cost of production. Thus the minimum of wages is the natural price of labour. And what is the minimum of wages? Just so much as is required for production of the articles indispensable for the maintenance of the worker, for putting him in a position to sustain himself, however badly, and to propagate his race, however slightly.

But do not imagine that the worker receives only this minimum wage, and still less that he always receives it.

No, according to this law, the working class will sometimes be more fortunate. It will sometimes receive something above the minimum, but this surplus will merely make up for the deficit which it will have received below the minimum in times of industrial stagnation. That is to say that, within a given time which recurs periodically, in the cycle which industry passes through while undergoing the vicissitudes of prosperity, overproduction, stagnation and crisis, when reckoning all that the working class will have had above and below necessaries, we shall see that, in all, it will have received neither more nor less than the minimum; i.e., the working class will have maintained itself as a class after enduring any amount of misery and misfortune, and after leaving many corpses upon the industrial battle-field. But what of that? The class will still exist; nay, more, it will have increased.

But this is not all. The progress of industry creates less expensive means of subsistence. Thus spirits have taken the place of beer, cotton that of wool and linen, and potatoes that of bread.

Thus, as means are constantly being found for the maintenance of labour on cheaper and more wretched food, the minimum of wages is constantly sinking. If these wages began by making the man work to live, they end by making him live the life of a machine. His existence has no other value than that of a simple productive force, and the capitalist treats him accordingly.

This law of commodity labour, of the minimum of wages, will be confirmed in proportion as the supposition of the economists, free trade, becomes an actual fact. Thus, of two things one: either we must reject all political economy based upon the assumption of free trade, or we must admit that under this free trade the whole severity of the economic laws will fall upon the workers.

To sum up, what is free trade under the present condition of society? It is freedom of capital. When you have overthrown the few national barriers which still restrict the progress of capital, you will merely have given it complete freedom of action. so long as you let the relation of wage labour to capital exist, it does not matter how favourable the conditions under which the exchange of commodities takes place, there will always be a class which will exploit and a class which will be exploited. It is really difficult to understand the claim of the free-traders who imagine that the more advantageous application of capital will abolish the antagonism between industrial capitalists and wage workers. On the contrary, the only result will be that the antagonism of these two classes will stand out still more clearly.

Let us assume for a moment that there are no more Corn Laws or national or local customs duties; in fact that all the accidental circumstances which today the worker may take to be the cause of his miserable condition have entirely vanished, and you will have removed so many curtains that hide from his eyes his true enemy.

He will see that capital become free will make him no less a slave than capital tramelled by customs duties.

Gentlemen! Do not allow yourselves to be deluded by the abstract word *freedom*. Whose freedom? It is not the freedom of one individual in relation to another, but the freedom of capital to crush the worker.

Why should you desire to go on sanctioning free competition with this idea of freedom, when this freedom is only the product of a state of things based upon free competition?

We have shown what sort of brotherhood free trade begets between the different classes of one and the same nation. The brotherhood which free trade would establish between the nations of the earth would hardly be more fraternal. To call cosmopolitan exploitation universal brotherhood is an idea that could only be engendered in the brain of the bourgeoisie. All the destructive phenomena which unlimited competition gives rise to within one country are reproduced in more gigantic proportions on the world market. We need not dwell any longer upon free trade sophisms on this subject, which are worth just as much as the arguments of our prize-winners Messrs. Hope, Morse and Greg.

For instance, we are told that free trade would create an international division of labour, and thereby give to each country the production which is most in harmony with its natural advantages.

You believe perhaps, gentlemen, that the production of coffee and sugar is the natural destiny of the West Indies.

Two centuries ago, nature, which does not trouble herself about commerce, had planted neither sugar-cane nor coffee trees there.

And it may be that in less than half a century you will find there neither coffee nor sugar, for the East Indies, by means of cheaper production, have already successfully combated this alleged natural destiny of the West Indies. And the West Indies, with their natural wealth, are already as heavy a burden for England as the weavers of Dacca, who also were destined from the beginning of time to weave by hand.

One other thing must never be forgotten, namely, that, just as everything has become a monopoly, there are also nowadays some branches of industry which dominate all the others, and secure to the nations which most largely cultivate them the command of the world market. Thus in international commerce cotton alone has much greater commercial importance than all the other raw materials used in the manufacture of clothing put together. It is truly ridiculous to see the free-traders stress the few specialities in each branch of industry, throwing them into the balance against the products used in everyday consumption and produced most cheaply in those countries in which manufacture is most highly developed.

If the free-traders cannot understand how one nation can grow rich at the expense of another, we need not wonder, since these same gentlemen also refuse to understand how within one country one class can enrich itself at the expense of another.

Do not imagine, gentlemen, that in criticizing freedom of trade we have the least intention of defending the system of protection.

One may declare oneself an enemy of the constitutional regime without declaring oneself a friend of the ancient regime.

Moreover, the protectionist system is nothing but a means of establishing large-scale industry in any given country, that is to say, of making it dependent upon the world market, and from the moment that dependence upon the world market is established, there is already more or less dependence upon free trade. Besides this, the protective system helps to develop free competition within a country. Hence we see that in countries where the bourgeoisie is beginning to make itself felt as a class, in Germany for example, it makes great efforts to obtain protective duties. They serve the bourgeoisie as weapons against feudalism and absolute government, as a means for the concentration of its own powers and for the realization of free trade within the same country.

But, in general, the protective system of our day is conservative, while the free trade system is destructive. It breaks up old nationalities and pushes the antagonism of the proletariat and the bourgeoisie to the extreme point. In a word, the free trade system hastens the social revolution. It is in this revolutionary sense alone, gentlemen, that I vote in favour of free trade.

EDITORIAL NOTES

1. Engels refers to K. Marx's *Letter to J. B. Schweitzer of* January 24, 1865. See present edition, pp. 136-141
2. See present edition pp. 52-58
3. Accountant of a government's chief revenue office. A fancy title used by Engels in a satirical sense.
4. An economist pursuing a definite tendency.
5. See present edition, p. 52
6. *THE POVERTY OF PHILOSOPHY. Answer to the "Philosophy of Poverty"* by M. Proudhon, is one of the most important productions of Marxism, Karl Marx's principal work directed against P. J. Proudhon, an ideologist of the petty bourgeoisie. The intention of criticizing Proudhon's views, which seriously impeded the dissemination of scientific communism among the workers, and at the same time shed light, from the scientific materialist position, on a number of questions of theory and tactics of the revolutionary proletarian movement, crystallized in Marx's mind in December 1846 as a result of his reading, a short time before, Proudhon's *Système des Contradictions économiques ou Philosophie de la Misère.* In his letter to the Russian literator P. V. Annenkov dated December 28, 1847, Marx propounded a number of important ideas, which later formed the core of his book against Proudhon. In January 1847, as appears from Engels's letter to Marx bearing date January 15, 1847, Marx was already at work on his reply to Proudhon. By the beginning of April it had been completed in the main and was in the print shop. On June 15, Marx wrote a short foreword.

   The book appeared in Brussels and Paris early in July 1847. Marx's followers saw it as a theoretical substantiation of the platform of the proletarian party which was taking shape at the time. While establishing contact on behalf of this party in the autumn of 1847 with the French socialists and democrats grouped around the newspaper *La Réforme*, Engels, speaking to Louis Blanc, one of its editors, called Marx's book against Proudhon "our programme" (see Engels' letter to Marx of October 25-26, 1847). Ferdinand Wolff, a member of the Communist League, published a detailed review of *The Poverty of Philosophy* in *Das Westphälische Dampfboot* for January and February 1848. The year 1885 witnessed the first German edition. Engels edited the translation, contributing a special preface and a number of notes to it. When editing the book Engels made use of the correct-ion in the copy of the French 1847 edition given by Marx as a gift on January 1, 1876, to Natalia Utina, wife of N. I. Utin, a member of the Russian Section of the First International. In 1886, the Russian Marxist Emancipation of Labour group published the first Russian edition of *The Poverty of Philosophy* in a translation made by Vera Zasulich. In 1892, a second German edition appeared. This too was prefaced by Engels, who here briefly corrected some textual inaccuracies. In 1896, after Engels's death, a second French edition of the book came out. It had been prepared by Laura Lafargue, Marx's second daughter, and also contained the marginal corrections in the Utina copy.

7. D. Ricardo, *On the Principles of Political Economy, and Taxation,* 1817.
8. The period in question begins after the termination of the Napoleonic wars and the restoration of the Bourbon dynasty in France in 1815.
9. The full reference is: Adam Smith, *An Inquiry into the Nature and Causes of the Wealth of Nations.* First edition appeared in London in 1776.
10. In the third edition of Ricardo's book (London, 1821) this part of the text is omitted—*Ed.*
11. In the copy Marx presented to N. Utina in 1876, after the word "labour" is added "labour power." This addition is found in the French edition of 1896.

12. Boisguillebert's work is quoted from the symposium *Economistes-financiers du XVIII siècle.* Prefaced by an historical sketch on each author and accompanied by commentaries and explanatory notes by Eugène Daire; Paris, 1843.

13. Troy is no more. (Virgil, *Aeneid,* 2: 325).

14. The full reference is: Th. Hodgskin, *Popular Political Economy,* London, 1827. The original mistakenly has here the name of Hopkins. In 1892, in the second German edition of *The Poverty of Philosophy,* Engels corrected this inaccuracy, which had been made use of by the Austrian bourgeois jurist Menger to make unwarranted assumptions about this reference by Marx.

15. The Ten Hours' Bill, which applied only to women and children, was passed by the British Parliament on June 8, 1847. Many manufacturers, however, ignored the law in practice.

16. The reference is to the following passage from Adam Smith's work, *An Inquiry into the Nature and Causes of the Wealth of Nations:*"In a tribe of hunters or shepherds a particular person makes bows and arrows, for example, with more readiness and dexterity than any other. He frequently exchanges them for cattle or for venison with his companions; and he finds at least that he can in this manner get more cattle and venison, than if he himself went to the field to catch them. From a regard to his own interest, therefore, the making of bows and arrows grows to be his chief business, and he becomes a sort of armourer." (Vol. I, Book I, Chapter II.)

17. Marx quotes a chapter from Voltaire's *Histoire du parlement.* It is entitled "France in the Period of the Regency and Law's System."

18. The reference is to Say's note on the French edition of Ricardo's book, Vol. II, pp. 206-207.

19. The latter reference in full is: Th. Tooke, *A History of Prices, and of the State of the Circulation, from 1793 to 1837.* Vols. I-II, London, 1838.

20. The first edition of the book was published in Columbia in 1826. A second, enlarged edition appeared in London in 1831.

21. The full reference is: M. Th. Sadler, *The Law of Population,* Vol. I, London, 1830, pp. 83 and 84.

22. The reference is to Quesnay's two principal economic works: *Tableau économique* (1758) and *Analyse du Tableau économique* (1766).

23. Marx hints at the work of Quesnay's contemporary N. Baudeau, *Explication du Tableau économique,* published in 1770.

24. G. W. F. Hegel, *Wissenschaft der Logik,* Bd. III; *Werke,* 2-te Aufl., Bd. V, Berlin, 1841, S. 320.

25. Marx quotes these words from the following passage of Lucretius's poem On the Nature of Things (Book III, line 869): *"mortalem vitam mors immortalis ademit"* ("immortal death hath taken away mortal life").

26. Marx refers to Chapter III, "Dela responsibilité de l'homme et de dieu, sous la loi de contradiction, ou solution du problème de la providence."

27. A. de Villeneuve-Bargemont, *Histoire de l'Économie politique,* the first edition of which appeared in Brussels in 1839.

28. In the copy with corrections in Marx's hand the words "du proletariat" ("of the proletariat") are underscored and the words "de le classe travailleuse" ("of the class of workers") are written in Engels' hand in the margin. These latter words are reproduced in the copy presented to N. Utina.—*Ed.*

29. Marx quotes Adam Smith's *An Inquiry into the Nature and Causes of the Wealth of Nations* from the French edition: *Recherches sur la nature et les causes de la richesse des nations,* T. I, Paris, 1802, pp. 33-34.

30. Lemontey alludes to his book: *Raison, folie, chacun son mot; petit cours de morale mis* à la *portée des vieux enfants (Reason, Folly, to Each His Own Word; a Short Course in Morality Within the Mental Reach of Old Children,* Paris, 1801).Marx quotes Lemontey's work *Influence morale de la division du travail,* in which Lemontey refers to the above book.

31. *Le Creusot* (Burgundy)—since the 1830s a big centre of the French metallurgical, machine-building and war industry; at the time referred to, the Creusot works belonged to Schneider and Co. founded in 1836.

32. The full reference is: Ch. Babbage, *Traité stir l'économie des machines et des manufactures,* Paris, 1833, p. 230.

33. The reference is to the first cyclic crisis of overproduction which began in England in 1825. The crisis involved all branches of industry, textiles in particular. it was followed by stagnation in trade, reduction of exports by 16 per cent and imports by 15 per cent and the insolvency of several banks.

34. Literally, in the countries of infidels. Here the phrase means: beyond the realm of reality. *In partibus infldelium* was an addition to the title of Catholic bishops appointed to purely nominal office in pagan countries.

35. P. Rossi, *Cours d'économie politique.* T. I-II, Paris, 1840-41.

36. James Steuart, *Recherches des principes de l'économie politique.* T. II, Paris, 1789, pp. 190-91. This first English edition of the book appeared in London in 1767.

37. Quoting from the French edition of J. Steuart's book published in 1789 (the first English edition: J. Steuart, *An Inquiry into the Principles of Political Economy, being an Essay on the Science of Domestic Policy in Free Nations* was published in two volumes in London in 1767), Marx made some explanatory additions and changes. Thus he added the words "impôt sur la production" (taxes on production), "impôtssur la consommation" (taxes on consumption) and the last sentence: "Chacun est imposé à raison de la dépense qu'il fait" (Everyone is taxed according to his expenditure). He changed the place of the sentence "Chacun est imposé à raison du profit qu'il est censé faire" (Everyone is taxed in proportion to the gain he is supposed to make), which Steuart has after "Ainsile monarque un impôt sur l'industrie" (thus the monarch imposes a tax upon industry). Instead of "le gouvernement limité" Marx used "le gouvernement constitutionnel".

38. The Man of Forty Écus—the hero of Voltaire's story of the same name, a modest, hard-working peasant with an annual income of 40 écus. The following passage is quoted from the story.

39. Literally, a god from out of the machine. In the theatre of antiquity actors representing gods appeared upon the scene by stage machinery to overcome a superhuman difficulty. Figuratively, a person who appears unexpectedly to save a situation.

40. *Propriété* [property] is explained by the intervention of the *propriétaire* (landowner); *rente* (rent), by the intervention of the *rentier* (rent receiver). Juxtaposition of *rente and rentier.*

41. In the copy Marx presented to N. Utina, the beginning of this sentence was altered as follows: "For the Ricardian doctrine, once the premises granted, to be generally true, it is moreover essential that..."

42. In the copy presented to N. Utina, the words "on inferior land" were altered to "on the land."

43. In the German edition of 1885 the last two sentences are omitted, and after "industrial capitalist" is added: "who exploits the soil by means of 'his wage workers, and who pays to the landowner as rent only the surplus over the production costs, including profit on capital."

44. W. Petty, *Political Arithmetick,* in the book W. Petty, *Several Essays in Political Arithmetick,* London, 1699.

45. The Corn Laws imposed high tariffs on agricultural imports in order to maintain high prices on agricultural products on the home market. First introduced in the 15th century, the Act of 1815 prohibited imports of grain when prices in England were below 80 sh. per quarter. Further Acts were passed in 1822, 1828 and other years. In 1838 manufacturers founded the Anti-Corn Law League to work for repeal of the Corn Laws. Acting for

"unrestricted free trade," the League sought to weaken the position of the landed aristocracy and also reduce workers' wages. The Corn Laws were repealed in 1846. See notes 28 and 47.

46. In 1836-38 a new cyclic crisis of overproduction swept over Britain and other capitalist countries.

47. In 1824 under mass pressure Parliament repealed the ban on the trade unions. However, in 1825 it passed a Bill on workers' combinations, which confirming the repeal of the ban on the trade unions at the same time greatly restricted their activity. in particular, mere agitation for workers to join unions and take part in strikes was regarded as "compulsion" and "violence" and punished as a crime.

48. The laws in operation at that time in France—the so-called Le Chapelier law adopted in 1791 during the bourgeois revolution by the Constituent Assembly and the criminal code elaborated under the Napoleonic Empire— forbade the workers to form labour unions or to go on strike on pain of severe punishment. The prohibition of trade unions was abolished in France as late as 1884.

49. *National Association of United Trades:* A trade union organization established in England in 1845. Its activity did not extend beyond the scope of economic struggle for better conditions of sale of labour power, for better labour laws. The Association existed until the early sixties, but after 1851 it did not play an important part in the trade union movement.

50. The term "instruments of production" is still used by Marx in a broader sense here than in his later works. Subsequently he drew a more strict distinction between "forces of production" in general and "instruments of production" as a component part of the former.

51. Engels had in mind first of all Ferdinand Lassalle who widely used the term "workers' estate" in his writings, in particular in his pamphlet *Arbeitepro-gramm* (Workers' Programme) published in 1862. The substitution of the terms "workers" or "fourth estate" for "working class" was characteristic of a number of other representatives of petty-bourgeois socialism.

52. "Combat or death: bloody struggle or extinction. Thus the question is inexorably put." George Sand, *Jean Ziska.* A historical novel. Introduction.

53. Published in the *Sozialdemokrat* of February 1, 3 and 5, 1865 "We considered it best to give the article *unuttered,*" stated an editorial note. See present edition, p. 7.

54. Marx, *The Poverty of Philosophy,* Chap. II. See present edition, p. 93.

55. Marx's speech *On the Question of Free Trade,* which appeared in French at Brussels early in February 1848, was translated into German the same year and published in Germany by Joseph Weydemeyer, a friend and pupil of Marx and Engels. In compliance with a wish Engels had expressed this work was printed in 1885 as an appendix to the first German edition of *The Poverty of Philosophy* and has since been reprinted repeatedly as part of that book.

56. See note 7, *l. c.,* I: 178-79.

57. Marx alludes to the Congress of Economists which was held in Brussels on September 16-18, 1848. The following, among others, were present from England: Dr. Bowring, M.P., Col. Thompson, Mr. Ewart, Mr. Brown, and James Wilson, editor of *the Economist.*

58. Speech in the House of Commons, July 28, 1835. (Hansard, Vol. XXIX, London 1835, pp. 1168-1170.)

59. Dr. Andrew Ure: *The Philosophy of Manufactures,* London 1835, Book I, Chap. I, p. 23.

NAME INDEX

A

Anderson, Adam (1692-1765)—30
Annenkov, Pavel Vasilyevich (1812-1887)—127
Arkwright, Richard (1732-1792)—103
Atkinson, William—51

B

Babbage, Charles (1792-1871)—101, 157
Bastiat, Frédéric (1801-1850)—140
Baudeau, Nicolas (1730-1792)—76
Blanqui, Jerome-Adolphe (1798-1854)—39
Boisguillebert, Pierre (1646-1714)—51, 66
Bonaparte, Louis—See Napoleon III
Bowering, John (1792-1872)—144, 146, 148, 150-51
Bray, John Francis (1809-1893)—9, 13, 52-56, 58, 143
Bright, John (1811-1889)—144
Brissot, Jean-Pierre (1754-1793)—137

C

Cabet, Etienne (1788-1856)—139
Charlemagne (1742-1814)—62
Charles II (1630-1685)—120
Cherbuliez, Antoine Élisge (1797-1869)—117
Colbert, Jean-Baptiste (1619-1683)—62, 107
Constancio, F. S. (1777-1846)—28, 35
Cooper, Thomas (1759-1840)—67

D

Daire, Louis-François-Eugène (1798-1847)—51, 66
Darimon, Louis Alfred (1819-1902)—143
Droz, François-Xavier-Joseph (1773-1851)—39
Dunoyer, Charles (1786-1862)—47, 139

E

Edmonds, Thomas Rowe (1803-1889)—9, 52
Eisenbart, Johann (1661-1727)—16
Engels, Frederick (1820-1895)—7, 16, 19, 36, 39, 58, 82, 106, 123, 126

F

Faucher, Lion (1803-1854)—121
Ferguson, Adam (1723-1816)—95
Feuerbach, Ludwig (1804-1872)—136
Fourier, Charles (1772-1837)—106, 123, 127, 135, 135

G

Gray John (1799-1850)—12, 13, 17, 19, 141-143
Greg, William (1809-1881)— 145, 146
Grün, Karl (1817-1887)—137

H

Harvey, William (1578-1657)—109
Hegel, Georg Wilhelm Friedrich (1770-1831)—76-7, 79-82, 127, 136, 138
Helvetius, Claude Adrien (17151771)—139
Hilditch, Richard—117
Hodgskin, Thomas (1787-1869)—8, 19, 52
Hope, George (1811-1876)—145
Huskisson, William (1770-1830)—123

K

Kant, Immanuel (1724-1804)—97, 137, 138

L

Lassalle, Ferdinand (1825-1864)—39, 158
Lauderdale, James (1759-1839)—28, 37, 70-71
Lemontey, Pierre-Edouard (1762-1826)—95, 104
Linguet, Simon-Nicolas-Henri (1736-1794)—140
Louis XIV (1638-1715)—65
Louis XV (1710-1774)—76

M

Malthus, Thomas Robert (1766-1834)—136
Marx, Karl (1818-1883) 7-10, 12, 19, 23, 39, 58, 127, 136, 141, 144
Menger, Anton (1841-1906)—19
Mill, James (1773-1836)—117
Mill, John-Stuart (1806-1873)—66

N

Napoleon I, Bonaparte (1769-1821)—82